Author

OF THE

SWIFT E

N EMPIRE

Title THE END OF L

WESTERN ROMAN *ation*

Class 937.

THE END OF THE WESTERN ROMAN EMPIRE

An Archaeological Investigation

Ellen Swift

First published in 2000 by Tempus Publishing Ltd

Reprinted in 2010 by
The History Press
The Mill, Brimscombe Port,
Stroud, Gloucestershire, GL5 2QG
www.thehistorypress.co.uk

British Library Cataloguing in Publication Data.
A catalogue record for this book is available from the British Library.

ISBN 978 0 7524 1478 2

Typesetting and origination by Tempus Publishing.
Printed and bound in England

Contents

Illustrations

Text figures

Colour Plates

Acknowledgements

This book would not have reached its final form without the assistance of a number of people, to whom I owe thanks. My greatest debt is of course to Richard Reece, who suggested that I write it, and who has been a constant source of inspiration and encouragement over the years. Richard Reece, Carol Peaker and Mark Schofield read parts of the text and offered useful suggestions and comments. Hester Swift kindly commented on the text and also carried out the laborious task of proof-reading the final copy.

Thanks to Andy Bevan, David Earle and James Conolly for assistance with the map illustrations, and to Niall for helping me out at the Society of Antiquaries.

I am also grateful to all the staff of museums and institutions which allowed me to reproduce illustrations from their collections. I must finally issue a thank you in the general direction of everyone who assisted with my thesis, far too numerous to mention here, on which this book is partly based.

1   Introduction

The end of an era is always compelling. At the time of writing this book, in 1999, there is a great preoccupation with the end of the second millennium. This prevailing pre-millennial tension is, of course, entirely arbitrary. As many people have pointed out, all the date really means is that approximately 2000 years have passed since the birth of Christ. Without the Romans, Jesus Christ would probably have remained an obscure eastern mystic, and his birth would go uncelebrated. The Roman Emperor Constantine the Great adopted Christianity in the fourth century AD and made it the official religion of the late Roman Empire. As a result, Christian ideas were diffused throughout Western Europe and the Mediterranean basin. Christianity became the dominant religion for centuries throughout Europe, and, through European colonisation, was in turn introduced in many other areas of the world. Had Constantine not encouraged and endorsed the new religion, it would have been unlikely to flourish in quite the same way. The Western world would not be getting over-excited about the 'Millennium' celebrations. The fact that Christianity became well established, and its ecclesiastical organisations were firmly in place before the collapse of the Roman Empire, is still having an ongoing effect on the events in our own lives. Immediately there is a direct link between what is happening today and the events of Antiquity.

To myself, studying the Roman period, it seems to me that the West today is still struggling free of the Classical World. A time traveller from the fourth century AD would undoubtedly be completely unnerved by most aspects of modern society, but he or she would find many small things reassuring and familiar. The architecture of many civic buildings, for example, with their Classical porticoes and pediments, and sculpture depicting events and people from Greek mythology. Suppose a late Roman time traveller were to visit a national art gallery. Not only would they be likely to find the façade of the building recognisable, but they would also have a ready knowledge of many themes in the paintings within. Until this century, paintings were overwhelmingly based on two sources: Classical mythology and biblical stories. Both of these sources would perhaps be more familiar to a fourth-century Roman than to the average twentieth-century passer-by in the street.

Sometimes it seems as if it is only yesterday that the Romans left. From this perspective, the remaining span of years between concertinas into a small space of time, into which it is difficult to fit the events of history. The growth and subsequent collapse of the Roman Empire is perhaps the single most significant event affecting the whole of Western Europe before this century. Despite the so-called 'dark ages' of early medieval Europe, the Roman Empire left a substantial legacy. We are just coming to the realisation that 'dark ages' may be a misnomer, and that the post-Roman West was a time of continuing development. Most areas of Europe were heavily influenced by their Roman past. Embryonic institutions from the late Roman period, such as the church, rapidly became cornerstones of the developing medieval world. (Orthodox church ritual in Ethiopia is still based directly on rites in use in late Antiquity, and the church, of course, still has considerable authority in many areas today.) Through this and other continuing influences, the Roman Empire is still visible in the modern world.

This book is about the end of the Roman Empire, and, paradoxically, also about its survival, through its influence on early medieval Europe. Certainly the events of the fourth and fifth century in the Western Roman Empire, and even the narratives about those events, have played a part in shaping the Europe of today. Many people who know nothing about the period have still heard of Edward Gibbon's famous book, *The Decline and Fall of The Roman Empire*, written in the eighteenth century. The 'End of the Roman West' has been retold many times from different perspectives to garner support for one or another political or religious regime; it will continue to be an important part of our own origin myth of Western Civilisation. Talking about the end of something may seem premature when we have not even touched on its beginning, but it is beyond the scope of this book to cover the whole of the Roman period. It may be useful, however, to provide a brief summary of a few significant events, and to discuss some evidence relating to the end of the Roman Empire, before moving into more detail on my particular approach to the subject.

Historical and archaeological background

In the fourth century AD, where this book begins, the Roman Empire was divided into two parts. By this time, neither part had much to do with Rome. The Eastern Roman Empire had its capital at Constantinople. It was preoccupied to a great extent with matters in the East, such as the Persian Empire just beyond the frontier. The Persians may not have received as much press as the barbarians of the Western Empire, but they managed to inflict the ultimate humiliation on the Romans by stuffing one of their Emperors who had been taken captive. We can only speculate on what they did with the resulting masterpiece of taxidermy. The capital of the Western Roman Empire was based wherever the Emperor happened to be in residence, for example at Trier in the Rhineland of Germany.

By the fourth century the Empire had undergone a transformation from earlier times in terms of both political organisation and culture. However, archaeology has added considerably to what we know about the Roman Empire in this period, and it does not look like a system in decline. Towns changed from sprawling settlements to tiny walled-in enclaves, but the prosperity of the land-owning classes can be clearly seen in the sumptuous villas flourishing in the countryside. Large cemeteries were established outside the towns, the main funeral rite having changed by this time from cremation to burial. There is evidence for the growing infiltration of Christian practices. Yet the establishment of Christianity, the new religion which was to be crucial in the decades after the Roman abandonment of the West, does not seem to have had a particularly damaging effect on older pagan practices and beliefs. Late pagan temples also flourished in some areas, with, for example, large ritual deposits of jewellery and other metalwork at many religious sites. Britain seems to have been a particularly wealthy province in the fourth century — more fourth-century silver hoards have been found here than in any other province. Its economy was on the up-turn at the time, and the pottery industries were booming, producing vast quantities of material.

In the Western Empire, one of the chief events of the period was the influx of Germanic tribes. These so-called 'barbarians' had, by the late Roman period, intermingled with the inhabitants of the Empire to such an extent that many Germanic soldiers occupied quite high-powered positions within the imperial administration. Other barbarians harassed the frontiers from without, sometimes taking the Roman authorities completely by surprise — it is a well-known fact that when the Huns swept through the Roman Empire they arrived before the messenger galloping to announce their invasion. The Eastern Roman Empire shrank somewhat but ultimately continued until the fall of Constantinople to the Turks in 1453. The Western Roman Empire is thought to have ended in about AD 476–80, depending on where you were in Europe.

For the most part, then, the fourth century was a time of cultural and political change, but it was also a time of established continuity. Roman provincial culture had fully developed, and flourished throughout the Western Empire, even in one of the most westerly provinces of all, Britannia.

Even from the perspective of late Antiquity itself, we cannot make an immediate and simplistic division between 'civilised' Romans and 'barbaric' Germanic peoples. Many of the barbarians were Christian by this point. They had been converted by enterprising Roman bishops and missionaries. (These conversions took place before the Romans had themselves agreed on the details of the new religion, which had the unfortunate effect of indoctrinating some Germanic groups such as the Visigoths with what later became heretical views.) St Augustine, writing from the relative safety of Roman Africa in about AD 413 on the sack of Rome by barbarian tribes, thought that the Christianised barbarians were an instrument of God's will, scourging the obstinate and reactionary pagans of Rome for failing to convert immediately to Christianity. The Christianisation of some Germanic peoples had the effect of creating divided loyalties in those such as Augustine. He saw the barbarian Christians, even though they were heretics, as less evil than stubbornly pagan Romans.

The partly 'Romanised' members of some Germanic tribes living within the Empire may have been just as significant in the end of the Roman Empire as those who were attacking it from beyond the frontiers. The Franks, in particular, settled in some numbers on the Roman side of the Rhine frontier, with the agreement of Rome. Did this have the effect of undermining Roman authority and culture from within? The Franks were probably among the more important Germanic groups concerned with events in the late Roman West. The differing impact of various barbarian groups is evident from the later written history and reputation of each tribe. 'Tribal' names, such as those of the Vandals and Huns, who swept through the Empire, but only managed to establish their own kingdoms for a short space of time, later became terms of abuse. The historical sources which refer to their presence, and, perhaps, the folk memory of the events themselves, obviously had a significant impact on later historians. 'Famous' barbarians such as the

Huns, however, may themselves have had no particular long-term effect on either the end of the Roman Empire or subsequent events in early medieval Europe. Their most important role may merely have been to displace other tribes, when they moved east from the steppe. The displaced tribes then went on to become key players in the final years of the Roman Empire and beyond. By contrast, the name of the Franks certainly did not become a derogatory term. Can we say, then, that they had less impact than the Huns and other Germanic tribes? Though 'Frank' did not become a synonym for 'enemy' (as 'Hun' later became), or for 'hooligan' (as 'Vandal' has become), the name did survive — and clearly shows their enormous influence. The Franks gave their name to France. This is most apparent in the German name for France, Frankreich. 'Franc' was also adopted as the unit of French currency in the eighteenth century. This usage reflects their greater achievements: establishing a kingdom and a long-lived dynasty. Their importance in the collapse of Roman authority and the establishment of early medieval Europe is assured. The Franks took over many aspects of Roman governance, and founded the Carolingian Empire which controlled much of Europe in the medieval period. Paradoxically, they might be considered as instrumental in both the breakdown and the survival of the Roman world.

The linguistic evidence shows the Roman impact on the Frankish successor kingdom, as opposed to kingdoms established by less Romanised barbarians. In Britain we speak English, a Germanic language descended from the languages spoken by the 'barbarian invaders', whereas French is derived from Latin, spoken by the Roman invaders. In this context it is interesting that there is no good evidence for surviving Roman or fifth-century churches in Britain whereas these are fairly frequent on the Continent. Roman bishops in France became the leaders of what was left of Gallo-Roman society, for example, becoming important political figures who mediated with the Germanic overlords. This can be compared to the importance, politically, of modern religious leaders such as Archbishop Desmond Tutu and the Dalai Lama. The Roman legacy to France, Belgium and many other countries on the Continental mainland was apparently much stronger than in Britain, a factor we will be discussing further in the final chapter of this book. However, since Latin survived through church use even in those areas which became Germanic speaking countries, the church was clearly an important factor in the preservation of the culture of late Antiquity throughout the post-Roman West.

How do we view the end of the Roman Empire from an early twenty-first-century perspective? The Victorians, and their contemporaries in other European countries, saw the Romans as a positive, civilising force, and liked to think of themselves in the same way. They therefore viewed the end of Roman rule, and the replacement of the Empire by smaller Germanic kingdoms, as an unfortunate regression. However, it is now often disputed that the end of the Roman Empire can be described as 'decline and fall' with the sense of moral, cultural and political decay from a dizzying height of civilisation, rationality and culture that this implies. Debate on the subject is still heavily influenced by Europe's colonial past, and by the demise of the British, Belgian, French Empire etc. There has been a move towards discrediting the empire builders of the recent past, and consequently, those of the more distant past as well. Since the Renaissance, Greek and

Roman politics, Roman military organisation and Classical art have been held up as the ideal. From this angle, the Germanic inheritors of the Western Empire, living in wooden huts and drawing without perspective, were naturally seen as 'fallen'. More recently, we have a less idealistic image of Rome, empires are seen as rather nasty, we are used to art that does not look like what it represents, and change rather than collapse is the favoured term. People still search for a reason, or reasons, for the end of the Roman Empire, but it is no longer viewed as a decline and a fall, merely a readjustment. It is disputed that the Romans were a Good Thing, and that the 'barbarians' were necessarily responsible for a regression into some kind of Dark Age Hell where people didn't wash so often and not so many of them could read books. However, thinking that the barbarians were a liberating influence on the oppressed majority in the Roman Empire is also dangerous. The Germanic tribes, with their warlike reputation, have been adopted as icons by many dubious political figures, including Hitler and Napoleon (who, in his 'Emperor of France' phase, had motifs embroidered on his ceremonial robes which were taken from the jewellery found in the tomb of the Germanic Frankish king Childeric).

Whether their influence was positive or negative, it is now thought that the numbers of 'barbarians' were actually quite small. If you didn't happen to be in the direct path of one of these supposedly ravening hordes, or were perhaps only exposed to Germanic people who had settled within the Empire and become an accepted part of it, would you have noticed that anything was changing?

The End through archaeological evidence

This is where archaeology comes in, as we try to assess the impact beyond any purely political goings-on. The evidence from historical sources forms a background of possibilities, but it remains the viewpoint of the élite. As already discussed, it has coloured the use of other types of evidence, such as the interpretation of archaeological remains. Archaeology is now increasingly being used independently to construct a picture of what was happening in the Roman world in the fourth and fifth centuries, the crucial period for those studying the end of the Roman Empire.

For some, the only immediate contact with the Roman authorities would have been paying taxes. A breakdown in Roman authority would probably have meant that you still paid a similar amount to the new people in control, but in a slightly less bureaucratic way. (They might just come and help themselves instead of waiting for you to voluntarily hand over some of your assets.) However, if there had also been a breakdown in the trade and marketing systems which were well established by the fourth century, due to the collapse of Roman authority and the end of issue of official coinage, you might also notice the differences in the availability of goods and services.

If the archaeological evidence is examined, certainly the end of the Roman Empire is visible in some respects. Things introduced by the Romans disappear, and influence from other cultural groups is clearly visible. In post-Roman Britain, for example, in the fifth century, there are no more Roman coins. There is no more wheel-made pottery, people forget about living in stone houses with heating under the floors, and Roman towns are left in ruins. Some small farmers, some of whom had begun to live in rectangular wooden buildings during the Roman conquest, reverted to their former types of house, used in the Iron Age: round huts. The 'Celtic resurgence' at the end of the fourth century has been much discussed. Forms of jewellery and styles of decoration that had not been common for 400 years reappeared at the end of the fourth century, and this trend continued in the fifth and sixth centuries, with an extraordinary flowering of Celtic art in manuscripts and on high-status metalwork. (The precise context of this supposed cultural revival must be investigated, and will be dealt with in more detail in the final chapter of this book.) The fifth-century presence of Anglo-Saxons, or people influenced by Germanic culture, is well attested from cemetery and settlement evidence; for example, people building wooden long houses like those found in northern Germany and Scandinavia. However, we must remember that some groups continued to live just as they always had, i.e. completely unaffected by the Romans, and unaffected by their disappearance. Many people continued to live in the same round wooden huts that they had always used before the conquest, *and* throughout the Roman period; the end of Roman authority certainly had no effect on them.

Even in the areas of the Empire which *were* significantly altered by the Roman invasion and their subsequent presence, we may be misled, by problems with the evidence, into thinking that there was some kind of immediate and dramatic collapse of provincial Roman culture, and that the gap between the supposed official withdrawal of the Roman authorities (between the end of the fourth century and the mid-to-late fifth century) and the subsequent establishment of the Germanic kingdoms (at the end of the fifth and later) cannot be filled. We think that we can see an absence of surviving Roman culture from the archaeological evidence as well as from the historical sources, but this may be a case of finding what you are looking for because you are looking for it, and because the historical sources have told you that this is what to expect. In fact, the evidence from this period must be considered very carefully indeed before we jump to any conclusions about what it might mean.

Collapse or continuity?

It has often been said that the lack of archaeological evidence from the fifth century is very striking and that there must have been an extreme disruption throughout the West, including a dramatic reduction in population, during the first half of the period. However, the supposed absence of material evidence might be more to do with archaeologists failing to recognise this evidence earlier in the twentieth century rather than it not existing at all. This has been shown to be the case for evidence of early Anglo-Saxon settlement, and might also be true of other types of fifth-century settlement. At the beginning of the twentieth century, for example, it is doubtful if any fifth-century settlement sites were known at all. However, important settlements, such as Yeavering in Northumberland, have since been discovered. The site consists of a very large enclosure with a complex system of buildings, and it has even been suggested that it was occupied by a royal household. Initial occupation appears to have begun in the early Anglo-Saxon period, and one building seems to have been an amphitheatre-type structure, modelled on a Roman original, but made from wood rather than stone. Other buildings are more Germanic in style, including characteristic sunken-featured buildings and other large rectangular halls.

It now seems obvious that sites with buildings made of wood are much harder to find and excavate than sites with masonry remains, and that this might help to explain the lack of evidence for the fifth century. The only evidence for wooden buildings is normally the post-holes which held the timbers; the rest has usually decayed completely. Because there was a change in building materials used, from a lot of stone or brick in the fourth century to wood in the fifth, archaeologists used to excavating Roman villas with plenty of brick and tile and mosaic floors failed to find the settlement sites of the fifth century. This explains the previous poor evidence for Anglo-Saxon settlements, if we can correlate Scandinavian and north German type 'long houses' with people from these areas. It must also be significant in the dearth of evidence relating to the remaining native 'post-Romano-British' population. Again, people who had been living in wooden houses before the Anglo-Saxons arrived, and who continued to live in them afterwards, would not have been noticed by archaeologists early in the twentieth century. They were both harder to find, and less interesting to our (questionably) illustrious forbears. Villas have lots of useful bits of tile and pot turning up in ploughed fields to tell you where they are, and they might have some mosaics or sculptures or gold (or something more exciting than the bits of animal bone from a smaller settlement of wooden houses). Similarly, Anglo-Saxon burial mounds and cemeteries might contain swords, helmets, and gold. Romans were supposed to live before AD 400, and Anglo-Saxons after this date. Villas were therefore found in the Roman period, and prestigious Anglo-Saxon cemeteries in the early medieval period. Fifth-century settlements, especially those of the remaining native population, were mostly not even looked for. Even if it did strike someone as a bit odd that no-one seemed to be living anywhere, though people were clearly dying, they were unable to identify the subtle evidence for settlements of wooden houses.

Now, of course, we can be superior about this regrettable bias, and go out looking for British settlements instead, from both before and after Britain ceased to be part of the Roman Empire. We can't be too smug though, because some of the errors which have led to assumptions of a 'Dark Age' in Britain and other parts of the former Western Empire are rather more recent; in particular, problems with dating the evidence we find.

Even in the recent past, sites have been placed by archaeologists in the fourth century, because the coins are late fourth-century, or we have preconceptions about the material being late fourth-century, or because we have a fixed idea that Britain stopped being part of the Roman Empire in AD 410 because one historical source says that it did. (Unless you are one of the people who believes that this particular written text, the rescript of Honorius, refers to Bruttium in Southern Italy rather than Britain.) Some sites which are currently being excavated, however, or which have been excavated in the last couple of years, and which have classic 'late Roman' artefacts and associations, are now more often being dated to the fifth century, or the crossover fourth-fifth century, rather than the fourth century. This shows the whereabouts of the supposedly 'missing' evidence for a continued Roman lifestyle in the fifth century. For many years, it has just been wrongly placed; wrongly dated to the fourth century.

Certainly official coin production in most areas of the Western Empire stopped at around AD 410, so if there are any sites which continued after this date they probably carried on using the old coins for longer, and not using new coins dating to the fifth century, which would have been easy for the archaeologists. Fourth-century coins appearing in graves with artefacts do not necessarily mean that the grave or the artefacts themselves date from the fourth century. This means we have to do it the hard way, by paying attention to how worn the fourth-century coins appear, and what types of other material are found on sites likely to date to the fifth century. Sometimes artefacts which have been considered to be of fourth-century date because of their associated coins and because of our assumptions about material which, to us, looks 'Roman' and therefore is assumed not to belong to the post-Roman period, can, with more experience, be shown to occur consistently on sites of a probably later date.

Artefact dating depends a great deal on typology. This means putting a collection of objects into chronological order according to the appearance of the objects. For example, since cars were invented in the early part of this century, they have changed considerably in appearance. Even if we didn't know the precise years when they were made, we would still be able to put them in chronological order purely by the way they look. Archaeologists do the same thing with artefacts from Antiquity, placing them in a sequence, and then using coin-dated graves, or other datable contexts containing some of the artefacts, to give an approximate date range for every object type in the sequence. Considering a fourth- and fifth-century typological series, since the dating evidence is scarce, there may only be one object in a coin-dated grave which gives the series its chronological starting point in the fourth century. If the suggested dating changes for one object, the dates of whole sequences of objects, which have been arranged chronologically, will also change. Objects which are re-dated from the fourth to the fifth century, as we recognise our prejudices about the material, therefore constantly push related chronological sequences further into the fifth century. Böhme surveyed late Roman finds in Europe, and suggested dates in the fourth and early fifth century for many types of belt fittings and other accessories, based on the relative chronological sequence of sites where they were found. However, ten years after his initial publication, he published a revised dating schedule for these objects which suggested that they were later than previously proposed, in fact mostly dating to the late fourth century and the whole of the fifth century. These differences may seem slight, but they have significant effects.

As archaeologists become more confident about assigning a fifth-century date to apparently fourth-century material, we find that there is not such a dearth of fifth-century 'post-Roman' activity as has always been supposed. A misleading picture has been created because the evidence has not been treated in a sufficiently sophisticated way. We find that the problem of where everything disappeared to at the end of the fourth century is partially solved by re-dating a number of sites which were excavated in the past and described as 'late Roman', while a closer examination of the material suggests that they may actually be of fifth-century date. There is some written evidence that suggests the continuation of the practices of the late Roman Empire in the fifth century. For example, Sidonius Appollinaris, writing in fifth-century Gaul, rambles on about old aristocratic families and rural villas as if nothing whatever has changed. He also complains about someone not having replied to his letter, and does not seem to think that barbarian invaders are enough of an excuse for the laxity of the postal system (though he also gives us some interesting insights into the Germanic ruling class).

Did ordinary people living in the fourth century know they were witnessing what has since been perceived as a cataclysmic fall? Changes in lifestyle and culture must have been far more gradual than has been assumed. Re-evaluation of the archaeological evidence shows that the end of the Roman Empire may have been incremental, especially in terms of a grass-roots change in culture and society.

It is obviously important to look at the fourth as well as the fifth century for evidence of the slowly changing Roman world that was eventually transformed into early medieval society. Now we have seen that there is not as big a contrast between material culture in the fourth and the fifth centuries as has always been supposed, we can look back to the fourth century with renewed interest to see how the material culture of the late Roman Empire was already changing in the fourth century, and how it reflects and contributes to military and civilian culture and society in the last years of the Western Roman Empire.

Using the archaeological evidence of objects

Most archaeology is about collecting vast amounts of data and identifying it. The next step is to attempt a plausible reconstruction of possible events from this data. When studying late Antiquity, the archaeology of one province is often discussed in depth, and academics take in a wide range of archaeological evidence, drawing attention to different aspects of the late Roman period such as changing patterns of settlement and fluctuations in manufacturing, for example the rise and fall of the late Roman pottery industries. The evidence is then used to construct their account of, for example, the End of Roman Britain. This progresses beyond the use of historical sources alone. Sometimes the information which can be gleaned from archaeology complements historical evidence, and sometimes it forms a completely different picture from that painted by contemporary observers, who all had their own motives for writing, and who were looking at events from the more privileged, literate end of society.

My aim is to add to the picture archaeologists are already building up by using the objects that are found on archaeological sites to investigate the people and society of the fourth and fifth centuries. I shall be concentrating specifically on the things that people wore, such as brooches and belt buckles, since this has been the focus of my research over the last few years. A large scale and detailed study of other object types such as pottery and glass would doubtless be equally productive. Though I will be using fewer types of evidence than the generic book on the end of any particular Roman province, I will be covering more ground — several different provinces which together formed a large chunk of the late Roman Western Empire. This will enable me to compare and contrast the evidence from different areas and to investigate key factors that vary from one region to another. Since clothes do not usually survive, studying jewellery and other dress accessories is one of the few ways we can look at dress in the past. However, the artefacts people were wearing and being buried with in the fourth and fifth centuries can also be used to investigate wider aspects of the end of Roman rule, and how it affected people's everyday lives.

The collection and study of objects in the past

Some of the most fascinating things about museum collections are the objects in them which have been known about for centuries. There are some artefacts in museums, particularly in Italy, whose history can be recorded right back to whose possession they were in the tenth century, and before that the family who owned them may have passed them down for generations. A British example might be the Crown Jewels. Although these are of course not of such great antiquity, it is known that the eleventh-century sapphire ring of Edward the Confessor is still present among them, incorporated into the Imperial State Crown made for Queen Victoria in 1837. The Crown Jewels and other famous treasures, though, are of course an exception; the vast majority of artefacts have at one time or another been lost, buried under the debris of the passing years, forgotten about, and then rediscovered.

The first people to become interested in objects as archaeological evidence were antiquarians in the nineteenth century. One Sunday afternoon, a gentleman cleric may have fancied a little stroll in the neighbouring countryside to help down a particularly heavy lunch, and might in the process have directed a few labourers to shift earth and find out what was under that peculiar bump visible from the library in the west wing. Having nothing much better to do (the parish helpfully attended to by the impoverished curate), the clergyman in question might then have spent many a profitable afternoon studying the objects which had been unearthed. This is the more desirable version of events, of course — plenty of distinguished gentlemen took off into other countries and looted choice pieces of antique sculpture here and there (such as the Parthenon friezes, whose return to Greece is currently being negotiated). Thankfully some antiquarians stuck to their own ground (literally). In the spirit of nineteenth-century discovery and exploration that prompted Darwin and others to go off round the world and record natural phenomena, many European gentlemen of leisure enthusiastically began to investigate their local surroundings instead. They made drawings of monuments still standing, and excavated others (usually still visible in the landscape, so sophisticated powers of detection were not required).

Nineteenth-century excavations of course left a lot to be desired, and it is unfortunate that some of the more striking tombs and barrows were not left intact until they could be more sensitively disinterred by today's or tomorrow's archaeologists. However it is surprising and impressive that even at this time many of the objects found were accurately identified and placed in the correct period. In quite a short space of time, antiquaries could, for the most part, accurately distinguish between Roman and Anglo-Saxon artefacts, and even between early and late Roman material. There are of course still some endearing admissions of doubt: one Frenchman titled his article in a nineteenth-century journal 'Bracelet en bronze portant des caracteres inconnus', which might be clumsily translated as 'bronze bracelet of unknown character'. It would now be recognised as a typical late Roman artefact. A number of beautiful illustrated catalogues and descriptions of material produced in the nineteenth century are still invaluable today for the information they contain (**colour plates 1-3**; see also **1, 2, 4, 16, 63, 69 & 70**).

The drive for pure discovery meant that the unearthing of objects and the production of illustrated books and catalogues was an end in itself. Objects were to be wondered over for their mystique, and their romantic connection with ancient times, rather than being sources of information beyond the obvious 'this is the kind of object the Romans wore'. Sadly, antiquarians in general proved not to be particularly good custodians of the material they found. Many objects ended up in museum collections without any details about where they came from. About a hundred years later, the study of objects has progressed enormously from identification and cataloguing, though these are still an important part of any study. Once the material is out of the ground and tucked away in little boxes in a museum, perhaps illustrated and described in a published catalogue, its potential is enormous. By drawing together vast amounts of material, looking for patterns, and then attempting to explain those patterns, we can study the detail of people's lives in the past, which in turn can contribute to a broader picture of events.

Problems with archaeological evidence

When studying objects, archaeologists have to be constantly aware of the danger that any spatial patterns found in the distribution of material may just represent archaeological activity rather than events in Antiquity. Archaeologists are learning, for example, to be sceptical of any concentration of metalwork finds in East Anglia. Initially, a noticeable concentration of Anglo-Saxon brooches in this area, compared to a sparser distribution through the rest of Britain, might appear to corroborate historical sources which talk about the area of settlement of Scandinavian and Germanic peoples. It might also be taken to support the place name evidence — Anglia, from the Scandinavian people, the Angles — which speaks for itself. However, it would be discovered on a trip to Norwich Museum that the counties of Norfolk and Suffolk were the first to set up a programme liaising with local metal-detectorists. For several years now, detectorists have been bringing in objects for recording, and contributing their own valuable knowledge, and the result is that not only do Anglo-Saxon finds appear in greater numbers here than anywhere else, but so do Roman brooches and many other types of finds. The finds brought in by those who have an interest in the past have therefore completely altered the picture of that past which has been painted from excavated sites. This is a useful reminder of how fragmentary the picture constructed from archaeological excavations actually is. The so-called 'portable antiquities' scheme is beginning to be set up in other areas also, and eventually the East Anglian bias may be corrected by a mass of material for other counties, which promises to be very exciting for archaeologists in general, and those studying objects in particular.

Some activities in the more distant past will also obscure the events we are trying to examine. Objects in museums, for example, will be those which were valued by the collectors at various times. Other objects found at the same time may have been discarded, given away, sold, or even melted down. Most people living in the past seem to have had a very pragmatic outlook about antiquities. This is evident from the way in which they cheerfully tore down parts of their houses which were hundreds of years old in order to keep up with the latest fashions in architecture and interior furnishings. It is only in the

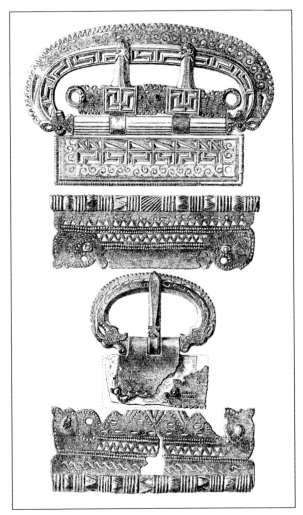

1 *Late Roman belt fittings from a German antiquarian volume, 'Der Altertumer unserer Heidnischen Vorzeit' (Antiquites of our Pagan Prehistory) by L. Lindenschmidt, Volume 1 (1858) Heft VI Taf 8.* Copyright Society of Antiquaries of London

twentieth century that an obsession with the past has developed, so that it is now fashionable to possess old things. Those living in the nineteenth century may have kept something only if it seemed valuable by the standards that were used at the time. Gold objects may therefore have been kept, and objects in other materials thrown away. It is important to be aware that the archaeological record is imperfect, and so are the techniques of archaeological research.

We must also take into account the changing uses an object may have had during its lifetime in Antiquity, before it was buried or lost. For example, items made from precious metals such as gold would be far more likely to be melted down and re-used in Antiquity itself, or, conversely, hoarded through many years and buried. These types of activities will all have an effect on patterns in the archaeological material. Although they do in themselves tell us something about the preoccupations of the makers and those who possessed the objects in later times, patterns such as these will tend to obstruct a clear picture of the period we are investigating.

Archaeologists have a habit of raising problems such as these and then going ahead with their investigations anyway. I fully intend to follow this admirable precedent. The alternative would be digging up sites and recording what has been found but not making any attempt whatsoever to interpret the material. The practice of archaeology will always be frustrating and imperfect, but knowledge of the past gradually becomes clearer with each new piece of research.

In the following chapters, the dress accessories and other material culture of the fourth and fifth centuries will be used to investigate specific groups who may have had differing identities — civilians in different provinces, foreigners, barbarians, the army — and, from this, to provide a new insight into the end of the Roman Empire in the West.

2 Dress, identity and regionality in the provinces

For some time now, archaeology has been influenced by anthropology, which, as well as recording dress customs and other practices, tries to investigate the reasons behind their existence. Dress has been used throughout human history as an important way of deliberately expressing specific identities. Even today people choose to distinguish themselves visually from one another by their dress, which is used to convey multiple messages at different symbolic levels. Objects can also be used and re-used in many different ways, and the original function of any dress accessory may bear little relation to its subsequent use and meaning.

Why do people wear jewellery? The supposedly 'correct' reason for wearing jewellery is to enhance your appearance, and to draw attention to a good feature. If you have nice hands, wear rings. A beautiful neck? Wear a necklace. Or more pragmatically, if the neckline of a dress doesn't suit you, wear a necklace to alter it. If you look a bit old and haggard in the mirror, some earrings will catch the light and make you look a bit better. Often though, these considerations don't even cross people's minds. Many people would perhaps say that they found the objects themselves attractive. What looks beautiful is of course open to interpretation, and in practice, people wear jewellery for many different reasons. Before launching into a study of the objects worn and used by people in late Antiquity, in the hope that this might be a useful new way of investigating the end of the Roman Empire in the West, it might be worth considering the way in which dress accessories are used in the present and the more recent past.

1 Fashion. Dress customs do not generally remain static over long periods of time but are subject to varying pressures, usually described as 'fashion'. It can often be a statement of affinity with a particular group, for example safety-pins worn in the seventies as punk jewellery, strings of 'love beads' favoured by hippies in the sixties, or Chanel pearls and gilt worn by well-bred, well-heeled or well-connected women for several decades. Fashion can also be linked to the 'zeitgeist' or spirit of the age at any one time. It is thought to represent wider social, cultural, political and even economic trends. The most well-known example from the twentieth century is of women's skirt lengths varying according to the economic climate. In the eighties boom, skirts got shorter and shorter, but plummeted with the following economic collapse. We can follow the effect of social and cultural trends on dress in recent history easily enough by looking at documentary sources and material culture together. For example, women wearing the so-called 'rational costume' — loose tops and bloomers — in the early part of the last century, rather than the dominant women's fashion of tight corsets and dresses which restricted their bodies and their movement. A growing awareness of the physical *and* social constraints women had been placed under, and their desire to reject these constraints, bringing in a new era or liberation for women, led to the development of the 'rational costume' and its adoption by women pioneering universal suffrage. Changes in ideas thus led directly to changes in the way a small minority of women dressed. Their contemporaries would immediately have known their political position from the clothes they wore. Eventually the new dress styles worn by these women, and other influences — such as the two World Wars — led to a complete transformation in women's dress over the next few decades.

2 Tradition. Folk costumes are most readily associated with 'tradition' and with the so-called 'ethnic' function of dress and dress accessories. Though traditional costumes are increasingly dying out, studies of different societies have been carried out in many areas of the world. Anthropologists have found that jewellery is sometimes used as a symbol of belonging to a particular group or region, especially in areas where one tribe borders another. In a series of anthropological studies of African peoples, Hodder showed that women sometimes wear particular items of jewellery or clothing, which specifically signify their membership of a particular ethnic group, when they visit an area occupied by another group, in order to distinguish themselves from the people living there. On returning home, they would not need to indicate their ethnic origin, as everyone would belong to the same group, and might wear instead garments which would distinguish their social position within their own tribe, for example those which functioned as markers of status and age.

3 Sentiment. Most people have some jewellery inherited from parents or grandparents, which they may keep for sentimental reasons even if it tends not to be worn very often. Couples, particularly, have appropriated jewellery as the symbol of another person. Heart-shaped lockets, which in the most nauseating variety are split so that the locket is only complete when the couple are together, are a good example.

4 Practical necessity. Medical lockets are worn by some people with potentially fatal illnesses. They contain details of the particular condition, and treatment, especially what *not* to give the person. In a slightly different vein, some people wear copper or magnetic bracelets which are reputed to have therapeutic properties.

5 Superstition and religion. Jewellery and dress are often used as a symbol of belonging to a religious or quasi-religious group, showing that the person wearing a particular item has a certain set of beliefs. Some jewellery of this type also functions as a good luck charm. Examples of dress accessories with religious associations are crosses and St Christopher medals worn by Christians, and yarmulke (small round caps placed on the back of the head) worn by Jewish men. Very orthodox Muslim women also wear distinctive dress concealing as much of the body as possible.

6 Symbol of specific status. The most obvious is wearing a ring to indicate that you are married or engaged. In the Victorian period, it was quite common for people to wear mourning jewellery, often made of jet, or with a setting containing hair. Together with clothing of black and muted colours, this informed people that you had recently suffered a bereavement, and could therefore not be expected to participate in the usual social rites, for example, dancing. More recently jewellery has been used by minority groups to signal a particular identity, such as, in the late eighties and early nineties, an earring in one ear (for men) being worn to indicate that you are gay. These types of symbols tend to change very quickly, so that only those on the inside recognise and understand their significance. They can also be appropriated from quite different contexts — thereby disarming any original negative connotations. A pink triangular badge, for example, is now a positive symbol for homosexuality, though, as is widely known, homosexuals were forced to wear this symbol by the Nazis.

7 General display of wealth and status. A good illustration of this, often cited as a peculiarly American practice, is the purchase of as large and ostentatious an engagement ring as possible, to show off the potential earning power of the husband and his presumed value for the woman in question. In the past, inherited heirloom jewellery would have been used in a similar way, worn by mothers and their eligible daughters to signal the wealth of the family to interested suitors.

8 Official symbols. Here the jewellery is made with a designated function in mind, for use within an official organisation. Examples might be military medals and school prefects' badges. Masonic symbols and badges — the apron, the wearing of one glove etc. — would mean nothing to those outside this organisation and are never worn beyond the Masonic hall.

Assessing all of these possible reasons for wearing jewellery, the most immediately striking thing is how many of them are associated with group identity, and how often jewellery is worn as a symbol of belonging to a specific organisation or cultural group. It seems that jewellery is never purely ornament, but always has other connotations.

A good case study illustrating developing symbolism in Roman dress is the gradual transformation of the toga and what it represented through the Roman republic and Empire, as discussed by Stone (1994) in the edited volume *The World of Roman Costume*. It seemingly originated as a purely functional wrap, certainly not restricted to the élite, but had already become a symbolic 'Roman' item of dress by the first century AD. As the toga continued to be worn it was decorated in various ways which indicated the rank of the wearer. For instance, a purple stripe along the border would indicate a magistrate or high priest. The everyday male toga retained the natural colour of the cloth, probably off-white. A mourning toga, of dark cloth, might also be worn. Togas were at their most popular during the first century BC and the first century AD, and during the later part of this time span, the Imperial period (when Rome had begun to be governed by emperors), they were already becoming a purely ceremonial item of dress. Practical alterations were gradually made, so that the draping could be held together more easily. However, this did not halt the toga's decline as an everyday item of dress and by the second century AD it had become purely formal or festive clothing. Modifications to the way it was draped around the body continued, and these changes can be seen in sculpture and paintings. (However, formal dress would be likely to have been worn for portraits, leading to an over-representation of the toga in the art historical record.) Although togas were still ceremonial dress in the fourth century AD, by the fifth century the sources show that they were replaced by military dress or court robes, which continued to develop in the Byzantine period. The toga continued to be worn, however, by priests, and gradually developed into the symbolic dress of the Roman Catholic priest. The history of the toga is an excellent example of the symbolism which can be attached to items of dress, and of how both the dress itself and its particular meaning may change through time.

How might the precise symbolism of dress and dress accessories be visible in the archaeological record? An example of jewellery being used to express a specific identity is mentioned above — the practice in the nineteenth and twentieth centuries of wearing a ring to show that you are married or engaged (i.e. you are not available to other potential suitors, and this is clearly indicated so as not to put these suitors through the embarrassment of having to ask). In the recent past, this custom applied only to women since at this time, it was supposed to be the men who did the choosing. Because of this, men would not need to wear a ring themselves. It was also accepted fairly widely that they had more sexual freedom than women, and, by implication, it would not be important to visibly mark their marital status. A man was not defined by his marital status, whereas a woman was, to the extent that this was deemed to be the most important thing you might need to know about her. (The male and female titles Mr and Miss/Mrs follow the same rules — the man does not have to reveal his marital status, the woman's is indicated clearly.) With a growing awareness of women's rights, women became uncomfortable with these implications. It is more common now for both sexes to wear rings, or, increasingly, for people not to get married at all.

Supposing that gold wedding rings were not removed at burial, an archaeologist in the future studying British skeletons buried today and in the recent past would notice that for maybe a couple of centuries (the unvarying custom did not settle down until comparatively recently) most female skeletons had a plain ring, often gold, on the third finger of the left hand, and perhaps an engagement ring on the same finger — typically a ring with a central setting of precious or semi-precious stone. In cemeteries which dated to a slightly later period — say the 1970s onwards — a ring on the wedding finger worn by both sexes would be the most common practice. Later still, the practice might become a minority one, or other more decorative rings would be worn on the wedding ring finger as it ceased to be reserved for symbolic expression. This shows how social trends can be represented at a basic level by objects in the archaeological record; whether the archaeologist would be able to draw the correct conclusions from the archaeology alone is the difficult part.

When studying the possible meaning of objects in the archaeological record, we have to be especially careful to establish that their position in a grave accurately reflects how they were worn in life, and is not just a burial ritual. A good example of how careful we have to be in interpreting burial practices is the convention of East-West burial, with head to the west, found in many churchyards and cemeteries and still continued today. The origin of this practice of E-W burials is the idea that you would be able to see the risen Christ at the end of the world when the dead rose from their graves. It could also have something to do with the sun rising in the east and setting in the west, and is unlikely to have had specific Christian connotations in the late Roman period, when E-W burial was also favoured. Certainly in the more recent past, though, this idea about Judgement Day enjoyed quite widespread currency, even to the extent that criminals would often be deliberately buried on a different axis, to scotch their chances of redemption. If you asked people today whether they believed in heaven and ultimately a bodily resurrection and a last judgement, even those who have no problems with the concept of an afterlife are perhaps unlikely to assent to a belief that your actual physical body will one day rise up from its grave. However, the practice of burying people E-W continues in many churchyards and cemeteries, following the alignment of the burials already there, those of people who may have had a more literal kind of Christian belief. It is difficult to distinguish the point at which the idea of physical resurrection was discarded. This illustrates a trap which we might be prone to fall into when interpreting the material evidence. It cannot be assumed that any burial rite we find in the archaeological record necessarily means that those buried believed in any spiritual/supernatural power associated with the particular rite, or were even aware of the meaning it may once have had, or may have had to the majority.

One of the most difficult things to deal with in the archaeological record, then, is that the symbolism of objects and rituals is constantly changing, though the objects/rituals themselves may still look the same. Though sometimes changes in symbolism may be identifiable through other evidence, such as the placement of the symbolic object, sometimes they will not.

Even the way that we ourselves view the objects of Antiquity is coloured by the unconscious symbolism which we attach to various things. An interesting demonstration of this is the way that 'crossbow' brooches (a type of brooch worn in the fourth century by officials and by the army), have been depicted in archaeological literature since this first began to be published. Crossbow brooches, as the name suggests, vaguely resemble a crossbow, or at least they did to whoever named them. Until very recently, they were invariably positioned as crosses in drawings (**2**), rather than the other way about, with the foot of the brooch at the top (**3**). It may perhaps have been tempting to wonder if the cross shape had any significance for late Roman wearers — after all, the late Roman army was a Christian army, after Constantine had been converted by a fortuitous victory in battle. However, placed in a cross shape they are in fact upside down, since we can see clearly from contemporary Roman illustrations that they were worn with the foot at the top. This foot is obviously visible, protruding above the right shoulder (see, for example, the illustration on the front cover of this book). They have conventionally been published the wrong way up.

In this case, it may be the inherent tendency of a western Christian upbringing to see cross-shaped objects as analogous to the crucifix, and, if one arm is longer that the rest, to place this towards the bottom. If a cross with unequal arms was placed with the longest arm towards the top, this of course was the sign of the devil — a cross shown upside down. (Reversing a 'good' symbol so that it becomes the signifier of evil is a very neat use

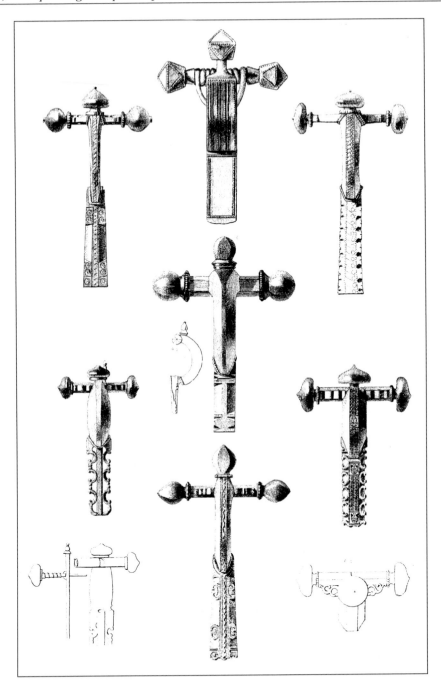

2 *Crossbow brooches, placed with the foot of the brooch towards the bottom, rather than
towards the top as they would actually have been worn, from a German antiquarian volume,
'Der Altertumer unserer Heidnischen Vorzeit' (Antiquites of our Pagan Prehistory) by L.
Lindenschmidt, Volume 3 (1870) Heft II Taf 4.* Copyright Society of Antiquaries of
London

3 A crossbow brooch placed with the foot at the top, as they would have been worn. Copyright Ellen Swift

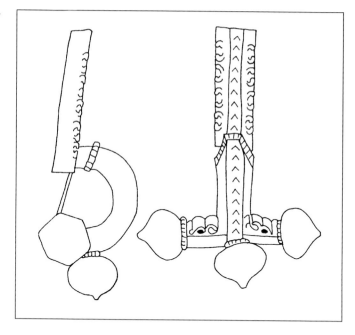

of symbolism.) These probably unconscious associations may have hindered considerably the early publication of crossbow brooches the correct way round. People may not have thought about it at all, but would have instinctively placed the brooch one way or another on the page before drawing it, and it must have seemed more 'natural' to place it as a cross would appear.

Working in a historical period such as the Roman era, we are lucky enough to know some things about the meaning of various symbols. The cross was avoided as a Christian symbol by the fourth-century Roman, perhaps because crosses had a connection with criminals and death (crucifixion was a frequent form of capital punishment). The cross shape of the upside down brooch would have a Christian significance only for an audience which understood it as a Christian symbol, and which had forgotten about its other associations. Early Christians were more likely to use the Chi-Rho (a monogram of the first two letters of Khristos, Christ, in Greek). This sometimes appears on grave monuments, for example, perhaps with other Christian symbols used by the Romans such as the peacock (**4**). The Chi-Rho motif does occur on a specific type of highly ornate gilt crossbow brooch, often together with portrait medallions which are usually thought to represent the Emperor (**5**). The symbolism of this decoration implies that in some sense the late Roman wearer of this brooch was authorised both by the Emperor, and by the Christian god.

Interpretation of the symbols and various decorative styles used by the Romans is not always this straightforward. However, although we may have problems finding out what the symbolism of objects in the archaeological record really is, I hope I have demonstrated that it is important to consider objects for what they may represent as well as noting their decorative appearance and the information they provide about dress customs and style in Antiquity.

4 Late Roman tombstone with Christian symbolism — peacocks and chi-rho motifs — from a German antiquarian volume, 'Der Altertümer unserer Heidnischen Vorzeit' (Antiquites of our Pagan Prehistory) by L. Lindenschmidt, Volume 1 (1858) Heft III Taf 8. Copyright Society of Antiquaries of London

Examining how jewellery is found in the archaeological record, there are some interesting trends which show jewellery being used in a complex symbolic way. We can begin to investigate the symbolism of objects by looking in turn at where they are found, how they were worn, and the details of what they actually looked like.

Ritual use and deposits

In the late Roman period, there was an increase in the practice of depositing bracelets and other jewellery at sacred sites. Roman temples and religious sites were often associated with water cults and goddesses. Making votive offerings to sacred springs and wells was a common practice, and many Roman temples have yielded rich deposits of coins, jewellery, statuettes and other material which was dedicated to the god or goddess of the sacred spring. People even tried to wish ill on their enemies by making a specific offering to the gods. For example, at Bath, curse tablets have been found, wishing an unsavoury fate on various hapless individuals. The Roman baths were a popular attraction in its heyday as a Georgian spa town, and the waters at Bath have continued to be regarded as possessing mysterious properties right up until the present day. Though people no longer deposit jewellery and artefacts in the water, coins are often thrown into the pools, while people make a wish — unconsciously acting in exactly the same way as the Roman occupants of the site.

At Lydney in Gloucestershire, the site of a late Roman temple of fourth-century date,

5 Late-fourth-century elaborate niello inlaid crossbow brooch with Emperor portraits and chi-rho motif from Basel. Redrawn after Laur-Belart 1959

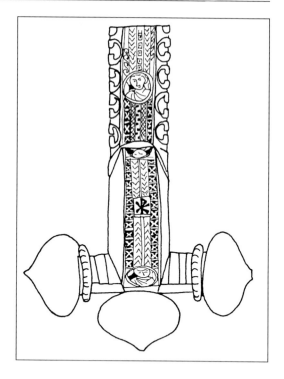

270 bracelets were found (**6**). Similarly, bracelets occur as part of a ritual deposit at many fourth-century temple sites in Britain and on the Continent. Woodward and Leach, who published the excavations of the shrine at Uley, suggested that particular objects were linked to different cults. They contend that votive jewellery is particularly associated with healing and fertility cults. It could be argued that there was an increase in the popularity of these specific cults in the late Roman period, reflected by an increase in deposits of jewellery at religious sites. However, a general prevalence of jewellery at temple sites in the fourth century might just be representative of its popularity as a dress accessory in the period.

Woodward and Leach even suggested that bracelets may have been made specifically for use as votive offerings. Many late Roman bracelets are simple strips of metal cut from a sheet and stamped with decorative patterns. They could be produced much more easily than objects such as statuettes and weapons. It is known from an inscription on the temple of Mercury at Yverdun in Switzerland that votive offerings were sold at temple sites. There is considerable evidence for smelting and metalworking at temples, for example, casting evidence and bronze ingots from Woodeaton, and a bronze smelting hearth at Lydney.

Some bracelets, therefore, may have changed in symbolic significance and function, first being worn by women in everyday life, and then deposited as a ritual offering. Conversely, perhaps these bracelets had religious significance while they were being worn as well as when they were deposited in a grave or at a shrine. Even more surprisingly, some bracelets may never have been worn at all.

It is also known that beads were sometimes worn as amulets in Antiquity, especially

6 *Flat strip bracelets with punched and notched decoration, just some of the 280 bracelets found at the late Roman temple site in Lydney Park, Gloucestershire.* Redrawn after Wheeler & Wheeler 1932

in areas beyond the Roman frontiers where beads were very popular among the Germanic inhabitants. Some archaeologists have suggested that more unusual types of beads found within the Roman Empire, such as jug-shaped beads found at Trier and elsewhere, might have been used as amulets as well. If this was the case, it would affect how they were manufactured and worn. Although most beads would not have had any intrinsic worth, as they were easy to make from cheap materials, once endowed with other nebulous powers they may have become of high value, which might have affected both how they were worn, and patterns of exchange and loss.

Dress and burial customs

In the fourth century burial without initial cremation was the usual rite, and large cemeteries often built up around towns. This is useful for archaeologists, as inhumation burials provide much more information about the dead than cremation burials. Concentrating on female burials first, there seems to have been a standard burial rite in Britain although more variation is apparent in very late Roman graves. Corpses were buried with an E-W orientation, wrapped in a winding sheet, without their clothes, and with jewellery and other accessories either not present at all or deposited separately in the grave (**7**).

If we look at cemeteries on the Continent, E-W burial without worn personal ornaments also seems to be the normal practice immediately across the Channel. However, moving further east, it seems to become more common for people to be buried wearing their jewellery, and bracelets are often found on the wrists of skeletons, a necklace is worn around the neck, and rings and earrings may also be worn at burial (**8**). It is usually presumed that this is how these objects were worn during the person's lifetime. There is no way of knowing for sure, and there may have been a convention of ritually dressing the dead

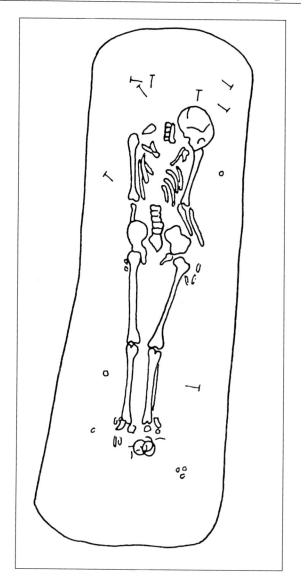

7 *Grave rite from the Lankhills cemetery, Winchester, grave 256: the usual provincial Roman practice of women's grave goods, including jewellery, being deposited in the grave, rather than being worn at burial.* Redrawn after Bignell in Clarke 1979

in a particular fashion (an example from the not too recent past would be burial in your Sunday suit or 'best' clothes rather than the clothes you would have worn every day). When the bones of a skeleton are studied, those wearing jewellery at burial, such as rings, bracelets and necklaces, or with these objects deposited in the grave, can invariably be shown to be female. In fact, they are often assumed to be female just from the jewellery, without checking the bone evidence, which is rather lazy and in a small minority of cases

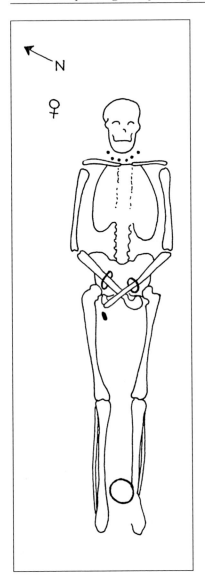

8 *Grave rite from the cemetery of Somogyszil, Hungary, grave 127: the predominating rite in the Roman province of Pannonia, modern day Hungary, and sometimes occurring in other provinces at the eastern end of the Western Empire — a woman buried wearing jewellery (and presumably clothes).* Redrawn after Burger 1979

misleading (unusual seemingly cross-dressing skeletons are a fascinating topic in their own right).

If we look at the evidence from Roman paintings and sculpture where bracelets are depicted, one bracelet is worn on each wrist. This seems to be how they were worn at burial in an increasing number of graves in Austria and South Germany. It appears that some people at least in these areas were being buried wearing their clothes and other dress accessories. Travelling as far east as Hungary, the differences from Britain in grave ritual are even more striking. Many cemeteries have been excavated in Hungary, and in the vast majority of them women are buried wearing bracelets. In some cemeteries the adult females are buried with only a couple of bracelets whereas the younger females have a number of bracelets in a row on the left arm. In other cemeteries, this difference does not exist (this may in some cases be a

9-10   Typical late Roman belt set and buckle found at the recently excavated very large late Roman cemetery at Ickham, Kent. Copyright Canterbury Archaeological Trust

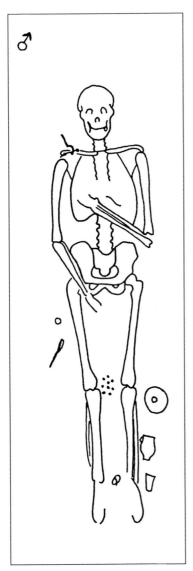

11 *Grave 33 from the cemetery of Somogyszil in Hungary, showing the most common 'military' burial rite of a worn crossbow brooch and unworn belt set placed at the feet. This practice was widespread throughout the Western Empire, though it occurs less often in Britain.* Redrawn after Burger 1979

failure to identify the age of the skeletons accurately). The rite is very distinctive and does not occur anywhere else, as far as I know, either inside the Roman Empire or outside its frontiers, in the fourth century or in any other period. As a result of this custom, hundreds more late Roman bracelets have been found in Hungary than in any other area of the Western Empire. Since, in some cemeteries, there is a difference between the women and the young girls, it might be speculated that the bracelets form some kind of marker of married as opposed to unmarried status. This would of course be useful for the male population, who were doing the choosing, as the provincial Romans were no more enlightened than anyone else. A visual distinction through body adornment between married and unmarried women is found in many cultures, not just those in the Western European tradition. For example, Bengali women rub a red paste along the parting of their hair when they are married.

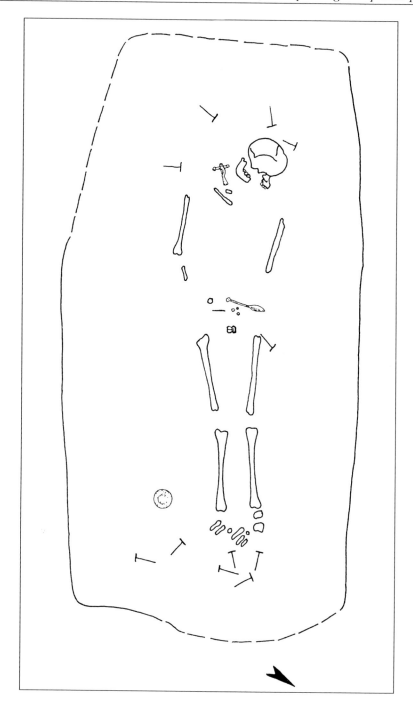

12 Grave 81 from Clarke's suggested foreign grave group at the Lankhills cemetery, Winchester. This man was buried with a more unusual 'military' burial rite, consisting of a worn belt set and crossbow brooch. Redrawn after Bignell in Clarke 1979

The fact that bracelets were used in this way in Hungary alone perhaps implies that those participating in this practice were a distinct cultural group. The rite does not seem to have an origin in the earlier Roman period in Hungary. If we examine Roman burials in the second century and earlier, the rite is not present. Neither is it found if we go back even further, to the pre-Roman culture of Hungary, and look at Iron Age sites from before the Roman occupation. The practice seems to appear suddenly in the fourth century, which perhaps suggests that it originally comes from somewhere else (although this is an easy answer often used by archaeologists to explain something they cannot account for). Looking for the most obvious source, and examining the cemeteries outside Roman Hungary, beyond the Danube (known as Sarmatia), again the rite does not occur. Sarmatian skeletons are often buried with jewellery, but this usually consists of large numbers of beads in coral, glass, carnelian and other materials, rather than bracelets. The bracelets which are found in these graves have obviously strayed from Roman Hungary, called Pannonia, rather than vice versa.

As is quite common with archaeology, the only definite conclusion we can draw is that a lot of the evidence which might point to the origin of this custom and its sudden appearance in fourth century cemeteries in Roman Pannonia must be missing. However, the way in which bracelets were worn in Pannonia is one of the more convincing examples visible in the archaeological record of artefacts being used in a way which seems obviously symbolic. When Pannonian girls were born, they may have been endowed with a large number of bracelets which were worn on the left arm, and which may have indicated unmarried or virginal status. When women married and had children, they might have passed on their own bracelets to female children, thereafter only wearing a couple of bracelets, which indicated that they were married women and mothers.

There is historical evidence of an analagous practice from the early Roman period (though this evidence applies to Roman rather than provincial costume). As Sebesta discusses in a piece on the symbolism of Roman women's costume, a female child would wear her hair combed in braids fastened with a woollen band. These woollen bands symbolised ritual purity and dedication to the gods. The child would wear her hair uncovered outdoors. However, on marriage, a veil would be worn for the wedding, and from then on the Roman woman would veil her head in public.

Returning to the fourth-century provinces, women, therefore, were buried with items in ways which vary according to where they happened to be in the Western Empire. It may or may not be the case that these items would have been worn in varying ways in different provincial areas, but it seems quite likely. We will examine later in this chapter some examples of different styles of jewellery being popular in different regions. There is also some evidence that other aspects of burial rite varied from one place to another, such as the high incidence of burials where the corpse was immersed in a layer of plaster (which have been argued by some to have Christian connotations) in Britain compared to other provinces.

We can also investigate the more precise symbolism of objects by looking at male graves. Like women, men buried in Britain are generally not wearing personal ornaments, and in some graves crossbow brooches and other items are deposited in the grave rather than being worn by the skeleton. There is, however, also a distinctive and widespread male burial rite used by the military, identified by Nik Cooke, which occurs sporadically in Britain, and more frequently in other places throughout the Empire, including Hungary. It is known that crossbow brooches, and belt sets (**9-10**) of some types, were used by the Romans to signify military or high-status civilian authority. Weapons, of course, are an obvious military indicator, and frequently occur in graves with belt sets. There are two main versions of a more specific military burial rite using dress accessories. In many graves, crossbow brooches are worn on the right shoulder, and a belt set is present in the grave, not worn, but placed by the site of the body or at the foot of the skeleton (**11**). In a smaller proportion of graves, both crossbow brooch and belt set are worn at burial, for example in a few male graves at the Lankhills cemetery in Winchester (**12**). Again this correlates with the evidence from paintings and mosaics of how these items were probably worn in everyday life. Where crossbow brooches are depicted in art they are always shown worn on the right shoulder. If the brooch is pinning the cloak on this shoulder, this leaves the hand which carries the sword conveniently free. However, for a left-handed person, the cloak might restrict movement considerably if pinned on this side. A significant minority of skeletons wear their crossbow brooch on the left shoulder, and these may be the skeletons of left-handed persons. Burials with the crossbow brooch placed on the left shoulder therefore support rather than undermine the suggestion that their placement in graves corresponds to how they were worn in life.

A very few crossbow brooches have been found in women's and children's graves in Hungary, for example at the late Roman cemetery at Sagvar. These are very much the exception, however.

The burial rite used by some men with military connections is therefore an easy way for us to recognise soldiers in the archaeological record. From the art historical evidence, and its coincidence with the burial practices, which we can examine, it seems likely that soldiers were readily distinctive from other citizens and people in the Roman Empire. Uniforms, of course, are an interesting thing in their own right. To state the obvious, they are worn to make people appear uniform. Why? A military uniform may convey the authority of someone else or something else apart from the wearer, and more powerful than him. A warrior in his own clothes and with his own weapons will only appear as threatening as his strength and tools permit. The same warrior, clad in a uniform which can immediately be identified with Roman authority, will carry all the weight of that authority as well — every rumour of military prowess, every tale of the ruthless efficiency and technical skill of the army as a whole. In short, the uniform depersonalises the wearer and gives him all the attributes of a collective body, such as the army. He will inevitably appear more intimidating, and the army en masse will have a much stronger impact. A uniform will also have an effect upon the wearer. He will feel as though he has something in common with other wearers, and will therefore be more likely to bond with them and feel loyalty and obligation towards his fellow soldiers. The Romans were certainly aware of the power of uniforms, with an elaborate code of who could or could not wear various colours and items of dress.

As well as being worn by those of rank in the military, crossbow brooches and belt sets were also worn by high-status officials, those in authority. If certain items are worn by those in authority, their badge of office will be an easy way to identify them in a crisis —

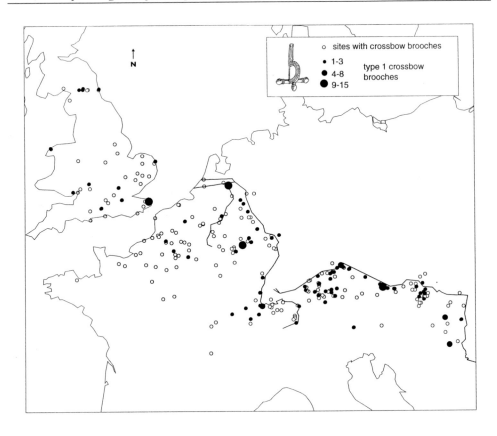

13 Map of crossbow brooches dating to the early fourth century (type 1) between the Loire and the Rhine/Danube, distributed mainly on military sites. Copyright Ellen Swift

another good reason for wearing a uniform. Not least, in an era when Germanic people were fighting on both sides of the conflict (both as members of the Roman army and as 'barbarian' warriors), it may also have been necessary to have some way of distinguishing your troops from the enemies, to avoid the tragic and over enthusiastic mistake of attacking your own troops in the midst of some blood-lusting frenzy.

There are, therefore, lots of good reasons why the army would find it useful to have a uniform, worn throughout the Empire, consisting probably at officer level of the military tunic and cloak, belt set and crossbow brooch. The crossbow brooch and cloak were also adopted by high-status civilian officials, much as the British royalty today wear military dress on some occasions, and are granted courtesy military ranking irrespective of their actual experience of combat. It follows that we should not be at all surprised to find soldiers buried in a distinctive and recognisable way throughout the Empire, all wearing items which are instantly identifiable. This widespread uniform again shows the use of objects in a specific symbolic way. The message is not merely 'I'm wearing a rather attractive brooch' but 'I'm a person with power and authority in the Roman Empire'. How that power and authority changes, and how it varied in different areas of the Western

14 Crossbow brooch of type 3/4 dating to the mid-to-late fourth century found at the very large late Roman cemetery at Ickham, Kent, which has been recently excavated. Copyright Canterbury Archaeological Trust

Empire, can therefore also be investigated by looking at these objects, which were such potent symbols of belonging in the Roman World.

A closer look at symbols of Roman status and authority

There are a number of types of crossbow brooches and belt sets. How do we know that they all had military/civilian high-status significance? Belt sets, for example, appear in graves without the distinctive military burial rite, as well as with it. Why do different types of crossbow brooch and belt set exist, if they were to be used as part of a standard uniform? Surely it would be more desirable to have identical brooches and belt sets for easy identification. Did military and civilian officials wear different brooches? Do the patterns which decorate brooches and belt sets have any special significance?

We shall examine in chapter four whether it is possible to distinguish between crossbow brooches worn by the military and those worn by civilian officials. Firstly, though, I want to consider the different types of crossbow brooches and belt sets in more detail, with a view to answering some of the above questions.

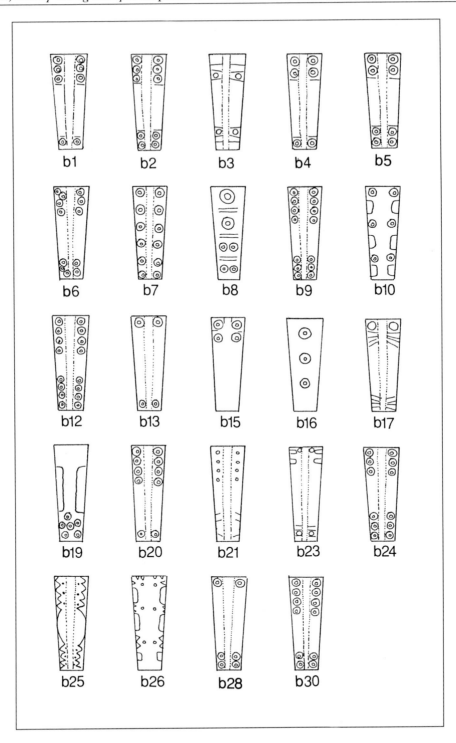

15 *Diagram showing the different foot patterns which are found on crossbow brooches with circle and dot decoration.* Copyright Ellen Swift

Crossbow brooches

Since crossbow brooches signify military/high-status civilian rank, it might be expected that they would be found throughout the Western Empire, or at least in areas where there was a military presence. When their general distribution through the Western Empire is examined, the association with military sites is strong. For example, the largest numbers of early crossbow brooches come from forts in Pannonia (Hungary) and on the frontier which ran along the Rhine and Danube rivers. Significant numbers have also been found at coastal forts like Oudenburg in Belgium and Richborough in Britain (**13**).

By looking at the patterns on these brooches and trying to find out where they were made, we can come to some particularly interesting conclusions about the differences between the Roman provinces which were situated on the frontier between the Roman Empire and free Germany, and those which were not, such as Britain and the west of France.

It has been suggested that crossbow brooches were all made in a military factory in Hungary. This was commonly proposed on several grounds:

1. The brooches were one item of more general military equipment and were therefore probably made in a military factory (the existence of such factories is mentioned in a late Roman historical document, the Notitia Dignitatum).
2. Most crossbow brooches look the same so they must have all been made in the same place.
3. Lots of these brooches seemed to turn up in Hungary, so this must be the place.

At this point, the reasoning is plausible, if not very sophisticated; it would be nice to have some more concrete evidence. I decided to test out the hypothesis by looking in more detail at the form and decoration of the brooches. The suggestion that they were all made in Pannonia and exported throughout the Empire is particularly important, as it has implications for the coherence of the late Roman army and administration towards the end of Roman rule in the West.

Crossbow brooches were originally divided by archaeologists into numbered types in a chronological sequence from type 1 to type 6. In any analysis of this kind, if there are several different types to choose from, it is always best to try to use the most common types. When you begin to divide the objects further, by more specific decorative features, if the original selection of material is too small your results may well be useless. You will often end up not being able to say anything at all, other than that while two brooches are like this, four are like that. This, it must be admitted, is not particularly ground-breaking.

First of all I separated out the most common type, the brooches produced in the middle years of the fourth century, called type 3/4. Crossbow brooch types were established by a German academic, Keller. More recently, another scholar from the same country, Pröttel, decided that, in practice, it was impossible to distinguish between type 3 and type 4 (he also added another type, type 7). The resulting type 3/4 is quite characteristic and easily recognised. (Rather than laboriously describing its features, which would not sound especially noticeable, consisting mainly of relative proportions of different parts of the brooch, I refer you to plate **14**). After choosing the most popular type, I divided the type 3/4 brooches based on the decoration found on a particular part of the brooch, the foot, restricting myself to the brooches with circle and dot patterns on the foot. To us, these circle and dot arrangements immediately recall the spots on dice, with circles arranged in opposing pairs, usually in even numbers. There are usually more pairs of spots at the top of the foot than there are at the bottom. I made a drawing of each different arrangement of dots which I came across (**15**), and counted the numbers of brooches with each arrangement. I then made a chart which shows the proportions of crossbow brooches with different foot patterns (using circle and dot decoration) occurring in each area of the Western Empire (**colour plate 4**).

There are several things which we can see immediately. Crossbow brooches get more similar as you go from west to east. The same foot patterns are most popular in each area. The three most popular foot patterns make up an extremely large proportion of the total in Hungary, which is the furthest east. Nearly half of the brooches found in Hungary have six spots at the top of the foot and four spots at the bottom. By contrast, the province furthest west, Britain, has the most variety, with small proportions of many different patterns, though there are still some brooches with six spots at the top and four at the bottom.

All this evidence seems to support the suggestion that most crossbow brooches were produced in Hungary. Since there are similar proportions of the most frequently occurring types in each province, we can suggest that they were deliberately exported to the other provinces. The patterns imply that the provinces on the Danube were virtually identical in terms of their military culture. The proportions of the different foot patterns probably has something to do with the quantity of production through time. Since Keller established that the later a brooch was produced, the more spots it has on the foot, we can use the proportions of different foot patterns with different numbers of spots to look at relative quantity of production through time. Production of type 3/4 crossbow brooches with circle and dot decoration peaked at the time of production of 4-6 spot, and then tailed off with smaller numbers produced which had two rows of spots running the whole length of the foot. Since this rise and fall is exactly the same in each province, it supports the hypothesis of production in one place and organised distribution for the most popular types. The other question, of course, is why was there a peak at a certain time? It could be related to the actual numbers of soldiers, or high-ranking soldiers who wore crossbow brooches, who were being recruited, or it could just relate to the time when the practice of wearing these brooches was most firmly established. Either way it suggests that in this particular period there was a lot of military activity.

However, the evidence also shows that something else entirely was going on in Britain and Western France. Here, the crossbow brooches that can be identified as coming from the factory in Pannonia are much less common. If we look at the distribution of the factory-made Pannonian brooches in Britain, that is the ones with the three most popular foot patterns which are found in very large numbers in Pannonia, it is found that they all cluster to the south east where imports would be most common, often occurring on coastal sites such as Richborough or Caister-by-Yarmouth. They do not make it further west or north, despite the fact that the north was the more militarised area of Roman Britain. Instead, the military in Britain and Western France seem to be making up their own foot patterns, and these are sometimes very odd — i.e different from the norm.

16 Elaborate chip-carved late Roman belt fittings from a German antiquarian volume, 'Der Altertümer unserer Heidnischen Vorzeit' (Antiquities of our Pagan Prehistory) by L. Lindenschmidt, Volume 1 (1858) Heft VI Taf 8. Copyright Society of Antiquaries of London

Other details of the brooches are also strange on closer examination, such as the shape of the terminals, and some of the other decorative features.

The kind of unintended drift in style which we have just investigated is easily missed, particularly by archaeologists who have only looked at the evidence from their own country, and unsurprisingly concluded that crossbow brooches all look the same. Then when they read in a foreign journal that crossbow brooches all look the same in France, too, they just say, ah, yes, that sounds familiar — and so the myth grows that they are the same everywhere and must all have been produced in one place.

We might now suggest that the importance of each area to the Roman authorities is reflected in the decoration on objects to be found in different areas. There is an obvious concentration of factory-made brooches, and by implication troops and money, in important defensive areas which were apparently under threat at this time (with barbarians periodically breaking through the Roman defences and, if the sources are to be believed, ravaging the Empire). Brooches may have been made in Hungary because they were most needed close by. The men on the frontier line were obviously present in large numbers and they were clearly identifiable as Roman soldiers, efficiently supplied from a probably military-run factory. By contrast, from the brooch patterns alone, we get a faint sense of a motley collection of undesirable remnants manning the garrisons in Britain, largely ignored by the administration, who did not bother to send them their official symbols.

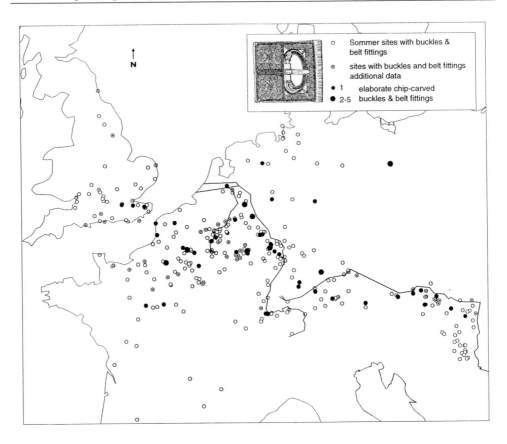

17 *Map of the distribution of elaborate chip-carved belt sets between the Loire and the Rhine/ Danube.* Copyright Ellen Swift

They then had to make their own, which of course became less and less convincingly 'official'. Only a few crack troops came over, bringing their good factory-produced brooch of standard appearance, but they lingered in the south east and could not be persuaded up north for love nor money. While this is of course speculative, there were certainly problems of supply to Britain and Western France at this time, or limited demand in these areas. The Roman army was not a unified force after all.

Belt Sets

There are a large number of different types of belt set, and many of these were in production at the same time. This might imply that they have a wide range of functions, and, perhaps, that not all belt sets were worn to indicate membership of a military or civilian élite. The only type of belt set which is actually referred to in the historical sources, and shown in contemporary illuminations as belonging to officials, is the wide, elaborately decorated belt set made up of many different pieces (**16**). As well as the buckle frame and the corresponding plate, attached to the frame, with rivets through it to hold the end of

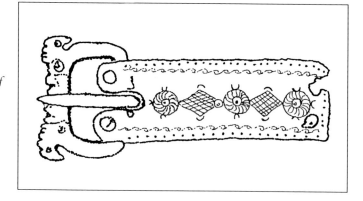

18 A double-sided horsehead buckle from the Anglo-Saxon cemetery at Dorchester on Thames. This type of buckle was undoubtedly made in Britain and is not found on the Continent. Redrawn after Hawkes & Dunning 1961

the leather, this type of belt set would also include other metal fittings. These consisted of a number of extra plates fitted along the length of the belt (some of them a distinctive propeller shape), perhaps an extra mount or two holding a loop from which various items could be suspended, and a strap end at the other end to the buckle. Decoration is always complex, a type of cast moulding in elaborate repeating patterns. The frame of the buckle is often ornamented with cast animals facing each other. Other belt sets are not obviously recognisable from contemporary illustrations, and are considerably simpler, often just consisting of a frame and plate, and perhaps a tag at the other end of the belt. They do not seem to belong to the same category of objects apparently made for ostentatious display. Though some do have careful engraving and inlaid decoration, and some are made from high-status materials such as gold and silver, many have much simpler stamped patterns (**colour plate 5**) and some were made for much narrower belts.

Were these types of belt set worn by the military as well, as has often been assumed? We might try to prove that they were by looking at the distribution of different types of belt sets to see if they are only found on military sites. At first this seems to be a promising approach. Belt sets made up of many pieces which are illustrated by contemporary sources are certainly found on a great number of sites along the Roman frontier and military roads, and have a bias towards these sites (**17**). Some other types of belt set also seem to be found predominantly on military sites, either along the frontier or at forts in other areas.

However, doubt is cast on the picture carefully under construction when it is discovered that some types of objects worn only by women — bracelets, beads and pins in specific styles — also have a distribution on military sites only. Opaque ring-shaped (annular) beads decorated with trails of wavy lines, for example, are found in the north-west of Britain (the north of Britain was predominantly a military zone), and along the military road between Bavay in France and Tongeren in Belgium. Their overall distribution on military sites is interesting, but difficult to explain. Beads with trail decoration are still found invariably in female graves, so it is not the case that men in the military are wearing them. Their distribution on military sites is also paralleled by some other female object types. For example, Hilary Cool identified a type of hairpin that only occurs on military sites in Britain. They, presumably, do not form part of any military uniform. By the fourth century, the set-up of the military has changed somewhat. An excavated fort of first or second century date would consist of cell-like barracks for a number of men, with the centurion having much larger quarters. A fourth century fort would be very different from this, with quarters for family units: men, women and children. Therefore a certain number of women presumably travelled with the army, though the arrangement would work best when men were recruited locally and never travelled very far from their initial point.

These examples show that civilian objects can also have a military distribution and that this alone does not necessarily imply a military function, though the distribution of some types of female objects on military sites alone is hard to explain. However, when considering male objects with a distribution on military sites only, it is questionable whether many civilian men would have been present, given that the soldiers were largely self-supporting, making their own tiles, building their own forts, and so on.

Sometimes, when we are trying to find out whether objects were worn by the military or not, there are also problems when we try to correlate how the object is found in the archaeological record with how it may have originally been worn, and by whom. It has often been said that a certain type of belt set found in Britain, a narrow plate and frame with backward-facing horses heads (**18**), cannot be military, as the type is sometimes found in female graves and does not occur in male graves. However, these horsehead buckles seem to be of mostly fifth-century date, and the fact that they do not occur on fourth-century military sites in male graves therefore means nothing. Their probable fifth-century date also means that we are lucky to find them in any contexts at all, given the problems associated with the fifth century, which I touched on in the first chapter. Most of the horsehead buckles that we know about are in quite elderly museum collections, and for the majority of these the original context has been lost, though we know the modern name of the town or village where they were found. A few horsehead buckles have been found in specific contexts in Anglo-Saxon cemeteries, often in female graves. We have no way of knowing, however, if this is representative of how the majority of these buckles were worn. We might suspect that it is not, given that Anglo-Saxon cemeteries are one of the more recognisable and well-documented types of site for the fifth century and later, and that there is therefore a bias to evidence from these cemeteries. They do not tell us anything about how the post-Romano-British population were wearing and using artefacts, and therefore do not show that horsehead buckles were not military.

These problems mean that at present it is impossible to reach any definite conclusions about the precise military symbolism of different types of buckles and belt fittings. It seems likely that some may have been worn only by the military, and some may have had wider usage.

Whether or not horsehead buckles are military or civilian, or both, one thing we can say is that horsehead buckles are definitely British. They are found only in this province, and throughout my travels on the Continent, visiting many of the most significant museum collections of Roman material in Europe, I did not come across one example of a horsehead buckle, although very recently one has turned up on a site in Spain. Conversely, Mark Corney, studying horsehead buckles from museums in Britain, found vast numbers of them. This brings up a new angle on the subject. How can these buckles be symbols of the Roman army, or more generally, Roman culture, when they are only worn by British people?

19 Silver multiple coin 'medallion' dating to AD 350 with mint marks showing that it was produced by the mints at Trier (TR). Copyright Ellen Swift

Decorative style in objects

Today we often speak of a global culture, ultimately based on American 'culture', which has spread to almost every part of the world. We have seen through the military burial rite that, among the military, there was to some extent a universal Roman identity throughout the Empire. However, crossbow brooches and belt sets differ according to which area you are looking at. Britain is different, perhaps because it is isolated from the Continental mainland. Female items of dress might be a good way to investigate whether these trends also existed among the civilian population. Evidence from dress accessories might reveal whether Roman influence pervaded the Empire to such an extent that everyone copied the fashions worn in Rome. Conversely, we can look at differing regional and local variations in jewellery. We have already seen that people in the different provinces had varying burial customs and perhaps different ways in which they wore jewellery in their lives. British buckles look different to buckles found on the Continent. Can we also distinguish between other types of dress accessories, which were worn in different provinces?

Some aspects of culture seem to have been the same in every province. Military dress and the uniformity or otherwise of military culture has already been discussed. Wild used relief sculptures on tombs to study civilian dress, and if they are a reliable portrayal of what people were wearing every day, it is suggested that by the fourth century everyone was wearing the same kind of costume, with a distinction of course between male and female dress. This was apparently not based on a Classical model — everyone had not started to wear togas — but instead was what we might regard as a more practical costume, based on leggings and some kind of overtunic for men, and a longer tunic-style dress for women.

Other universal fashions included the hairstyles depicted in busts and other sculpture,

20 A bronze coin with a date of AD 300-1 minted at Antioch, shown by the mint mark ANT.
Copyright Ellen Swift

and high-status gold and silver jewellery. These seem to have been much the same wherever you were in the Empire. Recently this has been illustrated in Britain by the discovery of two important precious metal hoards, the Snettisham Hoard, a collection of jewellery, metal scraps and coins buried by a jeweller in the second century, and the Hoxne treasure, a fourth-century find. The Snettisham jeweller had buried a number of silver snake bracelets of a type found widely in the Roman Empire. They had been assumed to be imports until this find was made. From the evidence of the Snettisham Hoard we now know that they were also produced in Britain, showing that the Romano-British were not quite so backward and provincial as had previously been assumed. The Hoxne hoard, buried a couple of centuries after the Snettisham find, contained some very typical, and universally popular, late open-work gold bracelets, which are easily paralleled as far away as Roman North Africa, for example in the Ténès hoard from Algeria. These examples show that at high-status level, people hundreds of miles apart would have found each other's dress familiar and therefore reassuring, with many identical dress accessories and probably the same general dress fashions. They were participating in a common culture, that of the late Roman world.

Even when investigating low-status jewellery (what is today called costume jewellery, implying that it has no intrinsic worth) and other dress accessories, the first point to emphasise is the notable similarity of dress styles throughout the area of the Western Empire covered by my research. Any cemetery or settlement excavated between Hungary and Britain will produce the same range of objects. These might include copper alloy (bronze, brass or gunmetal) bracelets, rings, pins, earrings, buckles and belt fittings, penannular brooches and crossbow brooches; glass beads and bracelets, and bone bracelets and pins. Some of these objects are very similar wherever they are found; some are noticeably varied in form and decoration.

Production systems and distribution

Workshops which are spaced widely apart in the different provinces of the Roman Empire are likely to show some variation in the types and styles of objects they produce. Following from this, it is often assumed that objects which are the same throughout the Empire were produced in one workshop and traded over long distances. The example of the snake bracelets from Snettisham, however, shows that this is not necessarily the case. It was thought that they were imported into Britain from the Continent until a jeweller's hoard was discovered in Britain which contained unfinished bracelets. From this, it can be concluded that although early snake bracelets were similar in all areas, they were probably made in several regional workshops. Can we distinguish between artefacts produced in one place, and those which are produced in several places but which copy one another?

The easiest way to look at this is by examining coin distribution. Coins need to be uniform, so that legitimate currency is easily recognisable. In the late Roman Empire they were produced in several mints geographically remote from one another. In this period, we can tell where each coin was originally produced because each was stamped with a mint mark. For example, coins made at Trier, in the Rhineland of Germany, would be stamped TR (**19**) and coins that were produced at Antioch, in Turkey, would be stamped ANT (**20**). Apart from these differences the coins would be produced to the same specifications, aiming at an identical design throughout the Empire. However, if we were to examine two identical denomination coins of the same date from different mints, although at a cursory glance the motifs would appear to be the same, on closer examination they would in fact have small differences in the design and in its execution, which would enable us to tell them apart even if they had not been stamped with different mint marks.

The same is true of jewellery, although in this case we do not have any production stamps which identify definitively where the objects were produced; some types of jewellery which at first appear to be the same throughout the Empire, such as cable bracelets made from a number of strands of wire twisted together, are not identical on closer inspection. Small differences, which correlate with different geographical locations, enable us to suggest that they have been produced in more than one place and distributed fairly locally. Different areas prefer bracelets with a different number of twisted wire strands, for example. The silver snakeshead bracelets mentioned above would probably also show some small variations of this kind among different regions. On the other hand, the presence of identical type 3/4 crossbow brooches, in the same proportions of different foot patterns, through Hungary - Belgium (leaving aside France and Britain which are different) with no regional variation at all, suggests that these type 3/4 brooches were indeed all produced in the same place and transferred to the various provinces in the same proportions. Other objects sometimes have very restricted distributions which indicate that they were made in a very local workshop and that they were only sold in the immediately surrounding area.

These variations in decorative style suggest that it is possible for the archaeologist to spot the difference between items which were produced in one place and widely distributed, those which were produced and distributed fairly locally in different designs, and those which were produced to the same pattern in different places.

Now we can move on to consider possible regional variations in female jewellery. We should be able to investigate production and distribution systems for different types of object and pinpoint jewellery which was made and marketed locally. We can find out if people in different parts of the Roman Empire were wearing different styles of jewellery, rather than following universal late Roman dress fashions.

Glass beads

Small glass beads in geometric shapes (cubes, cylinders, spheres, faceted cubes etc.) are found widely in the second and third centuries, and become increasingly popular in the fourth century (**colour plate 6**). They occur in such large quantities that they are obviously not expensive items. They would not repay the transport costs of long-distance trade. As they do not take up much space, they could have been traded alongside other goods which formed a main cargo. However, glass is a commodity which is easy to produce if you have the raw materials. These are common — all that is needed is sand, lime and soda ash, together with ready sources of water and fuel. Glass beads might easily have been produced in several different workshops, dotted around the West.

There are some kinds of beads that are only found in certain areas. Yellow square cylinder beads and blue hexagonal cylinder beads occur predominantly in the Danube area (**colour plates 7-8**). In general, white beads are found more frequently in Hungary, and less frequently in the other provinces of the late Roman Empire. White square cylinder beads in particular certainly have a strong association with Hungary. However, the most common beads found on sites throughout the West, from Hungary to Britain, occur in identical types and colours. These are cube-shaped beads with diamond-shaped facets, formed by rounding off each corner of the cube, and long hexagonal cylinder beads (**colour plate 9**). Wherever these beads are found, the cube-shaped faceted beads are invariably dark blue, and the hexagonal cylinder beads are most often green. As well as producing regional types, the workshop/s are also churning out beads which were universally popular throughout the Empire (**colour plates 10-11**).

How can we explain these patterns? Unfortunately, beads have a very small range of possible features that might vary. At present, it is difficult to identify visually, from small details, whether beads which look the same come from the same or different workshops. Comparing the exact colour of the beads found on two different sites is almost impossible, as people do not always describe colours in the same way, and what appears dark blue to one person may be simply blue to another. Photographs would be more helpful, but still not ideal, as colours in reproduction do not always come true. Colours may also have been affected by the deposition of the beads in different soils and conditions. In any case, it would be impossible to get all the beads found in the Western Empire together in one place. The answer might be to look at other more measurable features, measurable being the operative word. For example, you could measure the interior diameter of the hole through the centre of the bead, and if this proved to be generally larger in blue diamond-faceted beads that occurred in Belgium than it was in blue diamond-faceted beads that were found in Hungary, then it would be evidence that these beads, although very similar in appearance, were produced in different places. However of course we hit another problem here, which is that most archaeological research is done from published catalogues (compare the time and money it would take to go to every museum in between Budapest and Newcastle-on-Tyne, with the time taken to study publications held in nine or ten different libraries in Britain and the immediately accessible Continent) and it is unrealistic to expect those publishing the catalogue to go into as much detail as to give the diameters of the hole through each bead they find. Beads are often published extremely badly as it is, with even basic information such as colour and shape not always given for each individual bead. The day when an archaeologist has the time or the money to find out the diameters of the beads (or could cope with the boredom of doing this for thousands of beads) is therefore never likely to come. Another possible solution could be to analyse the chemical composition of beads. It is known, for example, that opaque glass made by the Romans contains different chemicals to early medieval opaque glass. The Romans used antimony to create an opaque effect, whereas tin was used in the early Germanic and medieval periods. This fact enabled archaeologists studying the Anglo-Saxon ship burial of Sutton Hoo to suggest that some of the glass objects found there were made from re-used Roman glass, as they contained antimony-based opacifiers.

Why, then, are some beads the same everywhere, while others show regional variation? Without the vast amount of extra research detailed above, which might provide more definite information, we can suggest three possible solutions to the problem:

1. Local workshops in each area are producing specific types of beads which have only a small distribution zone around the place where they were made. Meanwhile, one central workshop somewhere else is producing and exporting other kinds of beads throughout the Empire.
2. There is one central workshop, which produces all bead types. Yellow square cylinder beads are made specially to export to the Danube area, white ones to go to Hungary, etc. Other beads are exported everywhere.
3. Local workshops are making the universally popular types in each area as well as the less common types, which are found only in their marketing zone in one particular region.

Most obviously, the regional differences in bead types, together with economic factors such as the cost of transport and the easy availability of raw materials and technology, suggest to us that the third scenario is the most likely, with beads being produced in several different workshops, each with regional distribution zones for the final product. Although (2) could also account for the distribution pattern, it seems very unlikely. And (1) makes no sense at all — if local workshops existed, why would they allow a central production place to have a monopoly on certain types of beads? Why would the regional workshop in the Danube area be unable to produce long hexagonal green beads when they were making long hexagonal blue beads easily enough?

If beads were being produced by several different workshops, but, while some beads are the same everywhere, others are not, there must be something else at work which is influencing the types and colours of beads being manufactured. There seem to be both regional and Empire-wide preferences. We must try to explain why, from Britain to

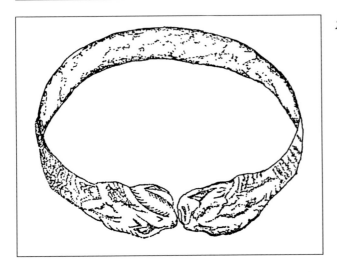

21 *Snake bracelet from the early Roman period. The snake is depicted with a degree of naturalism. These bracelets become more stylised over time, until they were almost unrecognisable as animals at all by the fourth century.* Redrawn after Verma 1989

Hungary, diamond-faceted beads usually occur in dark blue, and are very popular, though other beads vary in popularity in different places. As we have seen for the snake bracelets, the fact that diamond-faceted blue beads are the same everywhere does not seem to mean, necessarily, that they were made in one place.

In free Germany beyond the frontier, as Tempelmann Macyzynska has shown, diamond-faceted beads also occur in dark blue, and are popular. They are also found in other colours — green, white — and in other materials such as bone and carnelian. They were made and worn outside the Empire for centuries before they appear within it. What was once Germanic appears to have had no difficulty infiltrating and becoming popular throughout the late Roman world, so that it seems to us to be something that is a part of a universal Roman culture. The difficult topic of Germanic influence will be discussed further in chapters 3 and 5 of this book.

Perhaps it is possible to find a more specific reason behind the production of the other very popular type of bead found throughout the Western Empire — long green hexagonal cylinder beads. As I have already mentioned, a minority of finds from archaeological sites are of precious metal jewellery, sometimes set with precious stones. Necklaces of gold chain sometimes have emeralds in the chain. These emeralds are in the shapes of the naturally occurring crystal, a long hexagon, which would be by far the easiest shape for the jeweller to achieve in cut rather than polished stone. Green hexagonal glass beads are therefore attempting to reproduce the effect of precious metal jewellery, and it seems plausible that this is why long hexagonal beads are most often made from green rather than blue glass. High status emerald beads and necklaces cut in this way, part of the universal late Roman culture at élite levels, were mimicked by green glass long hexagonal beads throughout the Empire. These beads are not found beyond the frontiers; hexagonal beads do exist in Sarmatia and other areas beyond the Rhine and Danube, but they are characteristically a flattened hexagonal shape, easily distinguishable from Roman beads.

Other factors might also be significant in the choice of particular colours and shapes. The occurrence of white beads for example, might be associated with status. When glass is produced from raw materials, the chemicals present cause the glass that is produced to

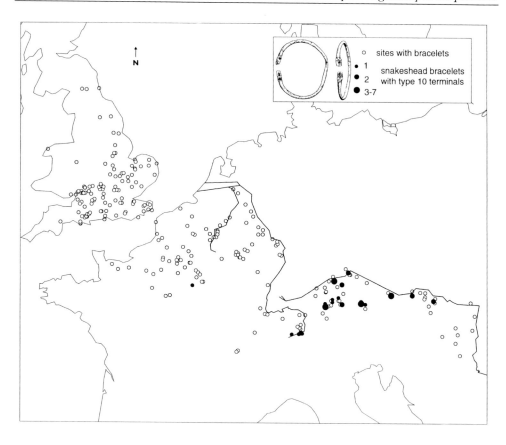

22 *Map of snakeshead bracelets with type 10 terminals (herringbone pattern) found between the Loire and the Rhine/Danube.* Copyright Ellen Swift

have a green-blue colour. In Antiquity, if coloured glass was required, it was fairly easy to add a colour to mask the natural green-blue hue of the glass. If white or colourless glass was wanted, the natural green-blue colour had to be removed, which was more difficult. White glass was consequently more expensive to produce than the other colours, and consequently more prestigious.

It can therefore be seen that a whole range of factors influences the types of beads found in different areas of the Roman Empire, and that production systems alone cannot be used to wholly account for the distribution patterns of different types of objects. The distribution and outward appearance of objects will sometimes, but not always, provide information about the scale of production, and perhaps the siting of regional or centralised workshops. However, production systems are in turn catering to the different levels of supply and demand for goods in each region.

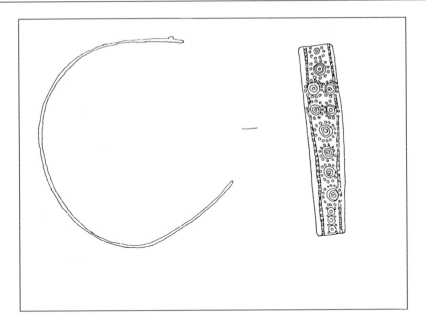

23 Late Roman rosette motif bracelet found during Napoleon III's excursions in the Fôret de Compiègne, France, and now in the Musée des Antiquités Nationales, St Germain-en-Laye, France. Copyright Ellen Swift

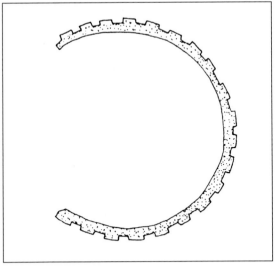

24 Cogwheel bracelet from the late Roman cemetery at Oudenburg. Redrawn after Mertens & Van Impe 1971

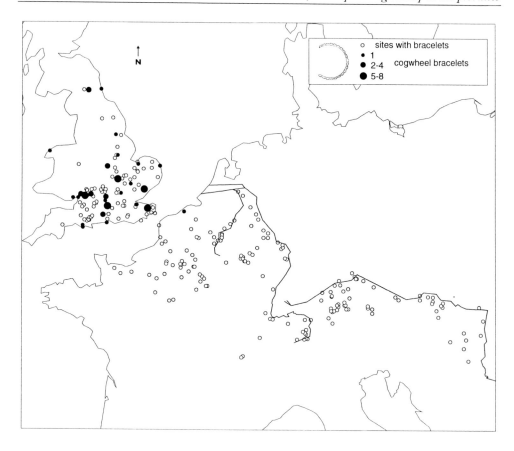

25 *Map of cogwheel bracelets found between the Loire and the Rhine/Danube; they occur on a single Continental site on the Channel coast and are otherwise found only in Britain.* Copyright Ellen Swift

Bracelets

Bracelets have a limited number of features: the overall form of the bracelet, the way it is fastened, the decoration along the front face of the bracelet, and sometimes any decoration on the fastening. As shown above, there are some bracelet styles which are widespread throughout the Empire, such as cable bracelets, present everywhere, though made in several workshops, each with smaller distribution zones. However, it is also apparent that the varied decorative styles of bracelets in different regions are very pronounced. There is an immediate and obvious distinction between the bracelet types which are found in the Roman provinces along the upper and lower Danube, the modern countries of Austria, Hungary and South Germany, and the bracelets which were worn in the areas now occupied by France, Belgium and Britain.

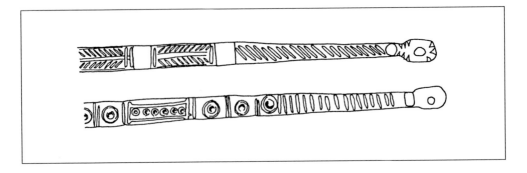

26 *Bracelets with multiple motif decoration found at the late Roman cemetery of Lankhills,*
Winchester. Redrawn after Griffiths in Clarke 1979

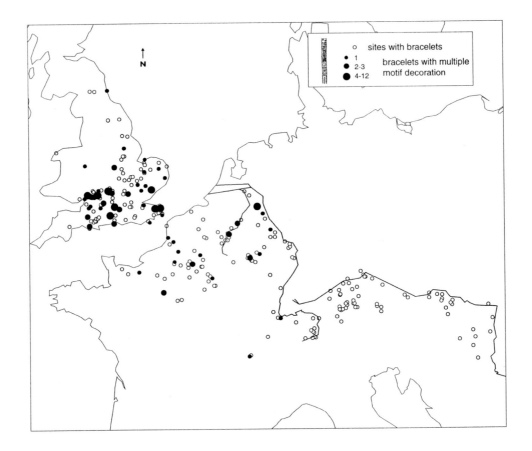

27 *Map of multiple motif bracelets found between the Loire and the Rhine/Danube; again the*
distribution is concentrated on British sites. Copyright Ellen Swift

Bracelets in the Danube provinces

In the earlier Roman period, bracelets in precious metals imitating the form of a snake were found throughout the Roman Empire, and in regions beyond the frontier such as Poland. The bracelet would be coiled around the wrist with the head of the snake at one end and the tail at the other, or sometimes in a two-headed version with a head at each end (**21**). These bracelets would not have a closed fastening, but just two ends and a gap into which you could slip your wrist. (This type of bracelet is called 'penannular'.) They were made from gold and silver and the Roman examples probably originate even earlier, from snake motifs in Greek jewellery. Snakeshead bracelets of very realistic three dimensional appearance, with added detailing of the scales, eyes and mouth, continued to be worn in each province in succeeding centuries, but gradually became less realistic. By the second and third centuries, a range of different snakehead bracelets were being worn outside the Empire as well, in the areas of Germany and Eastern Europe beyond the frontiers. It is thought that these were ultimately based on a Roman model. At the same time, in southern Germany and its environs, within the Roman Empire, bronze bracelets were being worn which had ends imitating boars' heads. In the Danube provinces, all of these strands of influence came together in the fourth century. They combined with the stylising tendency of late antique design to produce a large variety of penannular bracelets loosely based on the snake or animal head model (sometimes called more generally 'zoomorphic terminals'). Some of these bracelets are still recognisably animals — for example the muzzle of a beast is clearly visible in one type from south Germany — whereas in others the animal element has been reduced to the eye, a simple circle and dot stamp. As soon as you draw in the eye of the creature, you bring it to life, as one folk myth says. The eyes are the windows of the soul.

Some designs, particularly the more stylised snakes' heads, are found only in Hungary, whereas others occur only in South Germany and Austria (**22**). It seems to be the case that there were a number of different workshops which each produced snakeshead bracelets, fashionable throughout the Danube region, but made their own versions of them, which were sold in quite small local areas.

Bracelets in the Rhine provinces

In Britain, France and Belgium, this fashion for snakeshead bracelets did not continue beyond the second and third centuries in the same way, and they are relatively infrequent finds. Instead, Britain, France and Belgium all share the same preference for flat strip bracelets with a variety of designs stamped or incised on the uppermost surface (**23**). These range from simple incised lines and stamped dots to more complicated patterns of zig-zags and facets. Again, the evidence suggests that several workshops were in operation, each producing slightly different designs. Bracelets are particularly popular in Britain — as mentioned above, 270 were found at just one site, the Roman temple at Lydney Park in Gloucestershire. There are also some distinctive types of bracelet which are only found in Britain. The most recognisable is a type with cut-out sections which looks remarkably like a cogwheel. These bracelets are one of the most popular types found in Britain, but are not worn at all on the Continent — I only found one example outside Britain at the fort of Oudenburg in Belgium (**24-5**), which is on the Channel coast. A few have also been noted at Tongeren (Kathy Sas pers.comm)

The type known as 'multiple motif' bracelets are also extremely widespread in fourth-century Britain. They consist of a flat strip bracelet or a solid cast bracelet with D-shaped section decorated with panels of repeating motifs, usually symmetrically arranged (**26**). The motifs are invariably based on cut out zig-zag patterns and punched circle and dot decoration. The motifs which occur in individual panels are also found on other bracelets in Britain with simpler one-motif designs. At first, when I began to collect information from site reports about different kinds of bracelets, I thought that multiple motif bracelets were going to have the same distribution pattern as cogwheel bracelets. They cropped up time and time again in British site reports that catalogued materials found on excavations, but did not seem to appear at all in site reports from areas outside Britain. However, when I went on a museum trip abroad, I rapidly found that quite a few French and Belgian museums had a couple of these bracelets, though they did not occur in anything like as large a quantity as they did in Britain (**27**). Details of technique and fastening were identical, and, although bracelets with an identical set of repeating motifs are very rare, some identical pairs were found with one member of the pair on either side of the Channel — for example, one found at Rushall Down in Wiltshire is exactly the same as another found at Trier in the Rhineland of Germany. This evidence suggests that the bracelets of this type which are found in France and Belgium were also produced in Britain, but that they were either traded abroad or were carried there by the people wearing them. Since they are found on quite widely scattered sites, rather than being isolated at one or two places with other unusual material, it seems more likely that trade is responsible for their presence on the Continent.

Objects, then, can be used in a multiplicity of different ways to investigate the late Roman West. We can pick up an object and say where it came from by its decoration. We can investigate workshops and the scale of production of different types of objects, and look at trade and distribution systems. In turn, it becomes clear that though there were Empire-wide fashions in many object types, there were also numerous different regional preferences. Bracelets, beads, and belt sets all show a contrast between the decorative styles occurring in the Rhine and Danube provinces. Looking more closely at the crossbow brooches, which appear similar throughout the Empire, we can also see an opposition between the military culture of the Danube provinces on the main frontier line and those further away. This divide, and the relative isolation of Britain's material culture which has also been demonstrated in this chapter, was to become more and more significant in the final years of the late Roman West.

Sometimes the spatial variation in dress accessories extends to different dress/burial customs in different areas, for example, distinctive burial rites and material in Hungary. Here objects and the way in which they were worn may represent distinct cultural groups which existed in the late Roman world. They can be used to identify specific important groups, such as soldiers, or, in Pannonia, young women. Here we can see late Roman objects being used in the construction of identity. As shown in the examples from the present day, dress accessories have symbolic significance beyond their purely decorative appearance.

Objects can also be used to map the cultural changes from earlier centuries which had occurred by the fourth century — for example, the universal popularity of bead types which had once been Germanic; or the way that snakehead bracelets, once popular throughout the Empire, remained popular in the fourth century only in the Danube area. We can also see an increase in the use of jewellery for ritual purposes in the late Roman provinces.

If you can say where an object has come from can you say where its wearer has come from? This is what we will investigate in the next chapter.

3   People travelling in late Antiquity

From historical accounts, it is known that there was a great deal of movement in the late Roman Empire, principally the migration of barbarians, who travelled from their homelands on the edges of the Roman world. It is also known that the defenders of Empire, the soldiers in the army, were also sometimes transferred over long distances, travelling in some cases with their families. Looking for evidence of foreign travellers in the archaeological record, there are inscriptions from Hadrian's Wall which refer to soldiers of alien origin — an inscription at Chesterholm mentions Pannonia, for example. In this chapter several different sites will be examined. We may be able to find evidence both for people who travelled, probably with the army, from one area within the Roman Empire to another, and for the movements of Germanic peoples and other barbarians coming into the Empire from their homelands (often referred to as 'free Germany'). Firstly we have to find out where the objects that are found at a site come from, and then we have to assess whether they were brought there by their wearers, or got to the site by other means.

Scientific analysis of objects

Sometimes the original source of man-made materials, such as metals smelted from ore, and glass made from raw materials, can be investigated using scientific analysis. Consequently, we can find out where the object made of this material was produced. Glass, for example, tends to be of different compositions according to the elements present in local sands. One interesting study was carried out on second- and third-century beads by Boon. By analysing the different elements contained in the glass, he was able to suggest that transparent glass beads with gold foil in them found in Britain probably originated in Egypt. However, this method of analysis is not as useful as it first appears. The process of making glass or metal was quite inexact in Antiquity, and it is likely that two batches from the same production centre would have varying proportions of trace elements. Some elements vaporise at quite a low temperature and will be driven off. Those found in the glass or metal will not necessarily be representative of those found in the ore. The production of the final object from the raw material may also affect the composition of the metal or glass.

The most useful method may not be to look at trace elements, but at the internal composition of one element only, for example lead. Many chemical elements exist in more than one form, called isotopes. Each isotope has a different atomic mass, which depends on the number of particles inside each atom of the element. Many people are familiar with carbon-12 and carbon-14, which are different isotopes of carbon, C-14 being the radioactive isotope used for dating. Similarly, lead has several isotopes. Any deposit of lead ore is likely to contain a mixture of these different isotopes. When the lead ore is smelted to produce the metal, the proportions of the different isotopes will remain the same. The only way to change the atomic mass of an element (which often means that it becomes a new element altogether) is by a nuclear reaction as carried out in nuclear power stations. It will not be changed by the simple chemical processes needed for smelting. The proportions of lead isotopes in an artefact could therefore be compared with lead ore sources in various places to find out where the lead comes from.

A very interesting study of the lead contained in bones at Poundbury, a Roman cemetery in Dorchester, uses this method. Lead occurs in bones dug up from the ground for two reasons: firstly because of the small amount of lead which may have been present in the person's diet, and secondly, if the person is buried in a lead coffin the metal will naturally leach out and be taken up by the bones after burial. The lead present in most of the bones in the Poundbury cemetery corresponded to the lead ores found in the Mendip Hills nearby. However one rib bone contained, as well as the Mendips lead which will have come from their coffin, lead with different proportions of each lead isotope to that normally occurring in the Mendips. When compared to ores from many different areas of the Roman Empire, the relative proportions of the isotopes were closest to lead ore from Attica, Greece. Presumably, the skeleton with this lead in its bones belonged to a person who travelled from Attica to Dorchester.

Sometimes scientific analysis is inconclusive, as not enough metal analysis has been carried out in different places to find a possible source. However, by studying objects found over a very wide area, it has been established that people in different places were wearing different things. Some items or styles of decoration are found only in very small areas and in some cases we can suggest a region where a workshop for the production of a particular item might have been located. Scientific analysis can therefore be used in conjunction with stylistic analysis where we do not have enough evidence from scientific analysis alone. One example of this approach is a study of crossbow brooches from the Roman fort at Richborough, Kent, where a combination of evidence from metal analysis by Justine Bayley and from my own stylistic analysis shows that some of the brooches at Richborough probably came from the Danube area.

Stylistic evidence

Stylistic evidence can also be used in combination with other archaeological evidence, especially from grave contexts. Often, scientific analysis is too specialist and too expensive to be available to those writing up material. In theory, it should be possible to spot people who have moved from one area to another purely by examining the outward appearance of the artefacts they are wearing and carrying. Their jewellery and other dress fittings, and possibly the custom in which these are worn, will be different from that of the surrounding population. Once an unusual group of objects, whether from one grave or several graves, has been identified, we can look for an area where this type of object was the norm. However, it is vital that this evidence is considered carefully. Do objects travelling always mean people travelling? Obviously not, if foreign objects occur at a site in large enough quantities to be traded goods. The appearance of one or two items at a site is not always definitive either, but is more likely to be due to the movement of people wearing objects that they acquired somewhere else, especially if the objects are found together in a grave. The possibility of the craftsperson who made them moving or copying techniques from other areas must also be considered, though if items are copied by a local craftsman it is likely that small differences in appearance and technique will allow us to identify that they are copies of a style popular in another area, but made more locally.

It is important to carry out a detailed examination of the other evidence available. Once we are sure that some objects are foreign, we should also consider how many different kinds of foreign objects occur at the site, how many different graves contain them, whether more than one foreign object occurs in the same grave, and whether the graves which contain foreign material also have unusual burial rites, or are clumped together in the cemetery. Where objects do not occur in specific grave contexts, we have to be particularly careful not to make any assumptions. We must also think about the real-life experience of the people buried in these graves. It is far too easy for archaeology to become an abstract puzzle in which we ignore the realities of everyday life in Antiquity. It would be convenient for the archaeologist if people wore exactly the same things, items acquired in their homelands, throughout their journey, and then died still wearing the same objects. In the course of travelling many hundreds of miles, however, and perhaps living for some years in another area, there is likely to be some disruption, both of customs and material culture. Objects from another area may not indicate the original starting point of the travellers, but may have been picked up en route. We must also consider whether the visible differences in the archaeological record would also have been visible to the people wearing these objects, who would have been interacting with one another on a daily basis.

Foreign graves in the Lankhills cemetery, Winchester

Winchester was an important Roman town and the cemetery is particularly large and well furnished with grave goods. It is also well excavated, with an excellent site report. Looking at the practices found in the individual burials, the grave goods are mostly found deposited alongside the skeleton in the grave. The corpse would not wear clothes and dress accessories at burial, but would be wrapped in a winding sheet. This seems to be the normal practice in Roman Britain and much of the Roman world, as discussed in the previous chapter. Most excavated cemeteries of fourth-century date consist of burials with grave goods, where they occur, deposited separately.

However, the excavator of the cemetery, Giles Clarke, identified two groups of anomalous graves. The first was suggested to be very early evidence for the presence of Saxons in Britain, but the evidence presented by Clarke is rather ambiguous, and since most Saxon settlement is much later, in the fifth and sixth centuries, it is regarded with widespread scepticism by medieval archaeologists. The other group was more distinctive, and had what appeared to be a significantly different burial ritual. Objects such as brooches and bracelets were worn at burial (**12**), rather than being deposited separately in the grave. By implication, this means that clothes were probably also worn at burial, though these do not survive apart from a few fabric fragments adhering to some of the worn personal ornaments. Clarke also listed several other features of the burials which he thought marked them out from other graves at Lankhills. For example, in the whole group a vessel was placed at the right foot of the male skeletons and two vessels by the right foot of the female skeletons. Male graves often had a knife at the waist, whereas females' graves were provided with spindle whorls or combs. The male corpses were buried using the military rite identified by Nik Cooke, wearing a crossbow brooch and belt set. The rite is otherwise uncommon in graves in Britain. The female graves, however, were more unusual. The occupants were all wearing bracelets and bead necklaces, and in some cases a large number of bracelets were found on the left arm of the skeleton. As we have seen in chapter two, this custom is otherwise only found in Pannonia, at the other end of the Western Empire.

Is there any evidence that the objects themselves might have originated in Pannonia, or at least, outside Britain? Margaret Guido looked at the beads which made up the necklaces in the Lankhills graves. She found that some of the beads in the graves in Clarke's suggested 'foreign' group were made from amber and carnelian. In Britain, these are unusual materials. However, carnelian, amber and coral beads are common in Sarmatia, the area of Hungary beyond the Danube frontier of the Roman Empire. Guido also said that the flat hexagonal shape of some of the carnelian beads in grave 63 was characteristically Sarmatian.

Using the evidence from the burial ritual, and supported by Guido's independent suggestions about the beads, Clarke therefore proposed that the group of graves with worn personal ornaments could be linked to Pannonia or its neighbouring area, Sarmatia, and that the people buried in these graves had probably travelled to Britain with the army. This conclusion was disputed by some archaeologists, who said that the customary method of burial in late Roman Britain, with objects deposited separately in the grave rather than being worn at burial, was not the only burial rite used. They pointed to various sites with evidence for a range of different burial practices in late Roman Britain. It was suggested that the Lankhills graves were no more distinctive than others richly provided with grave goods, and that this particular practice was on the increase in Britain generally towards the end of the fourth century.

However, this fails to account for the unusual materials used for some of the beads, and, with the recent publication of several large cemetery reports, it remains the case that burials with worn personal ornaments are not very common in late Roman Britain. Examining the other beads (those made from glass), and the buckles present in the male graves, I found that two male graves in Clarke's suggested 'foreign' group

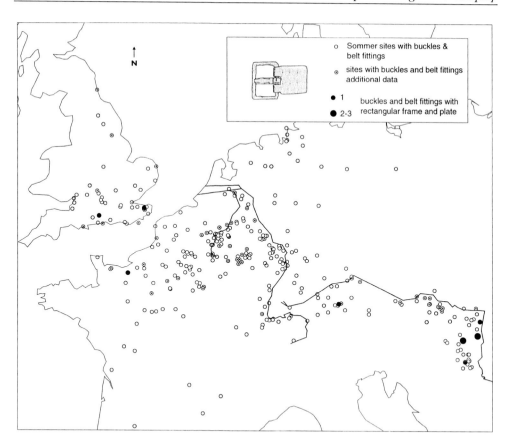

*28 Map of buckles with rectangular frame and plate found on sites between the Loire and the Rhine/
Danube.* Copyright Ellen Swift

contained buckles of a type which are not at all common in Britain. One of these, from
grave 234, is the rectangular buckle type which is otherwise found predominantly in the
Roman provinces of Pannonia (Hungary east of the Danube) and Dalmatia (in the area of
the former Yugoslavia) (**28**). The only other rectangular buckle dating to the late Roman
period in Britain, to my knowledge, is one at Canterbury. This is interesting, as there
is some other evidence from Canterbury of a similar burial rite to that in the Lankhills
cemetery, though different reasons- deposition in a pit rather than formal burial- could
possibly lie behind it. An extremely unusual burial was found in Stour Street: a large pit
contained the remains of several skeletons, probably a family group (**colour plate 12**).
The female skeletons had beads and bracelets worn at burial, including one with a lot of
bracelets on the left wrist (**colour plate 13**). In this case, the grave goods have not yet
been published, and therefore I cannot comment on them directly, though some seem to
be unusual. A woman with many bracelets on the left wrist was also found in the Diocesan
House excavations in Canterbury. Other finds have turned up in Canterbury which come

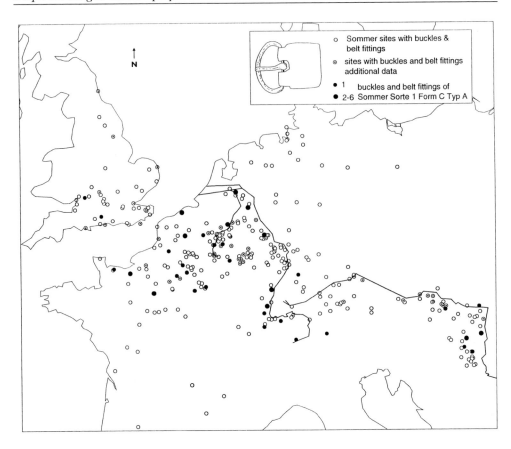

29 Map of buckles with unornamented D-shaped frame and rectangular plate (Sommer's Sorte 1 Form C Typ A) found on sites between the Loire and the Rhine/Danube. Copyright Ellen Swift

from Pannonia or the Danube area; as well as the rectangular buckle, a fragment of a bracelet with wrapped terminals has been found which is typical of this area.

Returning to the Lankhills graves, drop-shaped green beads and green diamond-faceted beads, which were found in the female graves in the group, are also very unusual in Britain. Diamond-faceted green beads are not particularly common anywhere within the Empire. My study only covers in detail material found inside the Empire, but looking at other evidence, from a study by Tempelmann-Maczynska, green diamond-faceted beads are found beyond the frontiers, and cluster around the north sea coast in free Germany. Drop-shaped beads in various colours are also not very frequent finds within the Empire, but they are found in Pannonia.

On firmer ground, since numbers are larger, hexagonal blue cylinder beads found in graves 336 and 323 do not occur anywhere else in Britain, and from my research are only found at sites along the frontier line on the Danube (**colour plate 8**).

Looking at the burial rite more closely, a distinction can be made between the bracelets

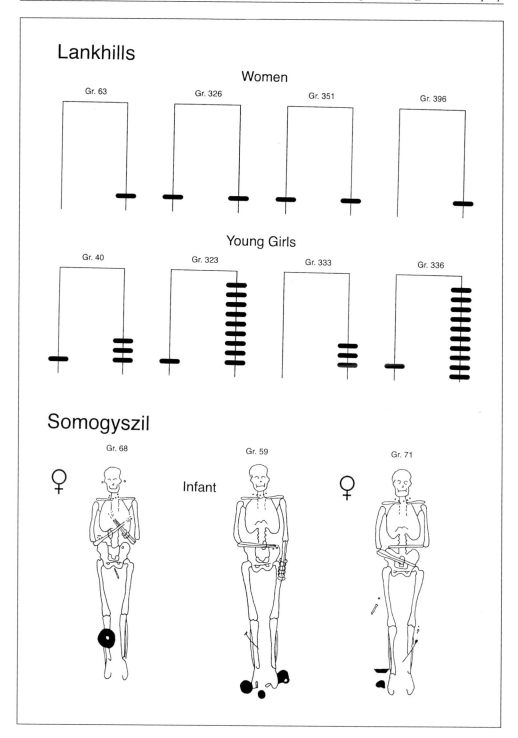

30 *Burials of women and juveniles with bracelets worn at burial from Lankhills, Winchester and Somogyszil, Hungary.* Copyright Ellen Swift

worn by the adult females and those worn by younger women. The younger women are the ones who have many bracelets on the left wrist; the adult females only have one or two bracelets on the left wrist, and sometimes one on the right wrist. Again, this correlates precisely with some Pannonian cemeteries such as Somogyzil, discussed earlier, where it is only the younger women who have large numbers of bracelets (**30**).

The following evidence can now be brought together for the Lankhills foreign grave group:

Grave rite of worn personal ornaments including many bracelets on the left arm (usual rite in Pannonia) and other consistent placement of grave goods as noted by Clarke: Graves 13, 23, 40, 63, 81, 106, 234, 322, 323, 326, 333, 336, 351, 366, 396, & 426.

Graves 40, 63, 323, 326, 333, 336, 351 & 396 Different numbers of bracelets worn by young girls as opposed to adult females — girls wear a lot of bracelets, and adults only a few (common burial practice only in Pannonia).

GRAVE 106 Buckle with D-shaped frame and rectangular plate (not common in Britain).

GRAVE 234 Buckle with rectangular frame and rectangular plate (otherwise found in Pannonia and regions further east).

GRAVE 336 Hexagonal blue cylinder beads (found only on the Danube frontier line). Drop-shaped green bead (found in Pannonia), heart-shaped blue bead (most common in northern Gaul), amber bead (suggested by Guido to come from beyond the frontier). Bone diamond-faceted beads.

GRAVE 323 Hexagonal blue cylinder beads from the Danube area as above, plus diamond-faceted green beads, which are not common within the Empire but do occur outside it. One amber bead, which may come from beyond the frontier.

GRAVE 326 Diamond-faceted green beads, uncommon within the Empire, especially in Britain, as above.

GRAVE 63 Carnelian diamond-faceted beads and carnelian flat hexagonal beads, suggested by Guido to come from Sarmatia.

All of these unusual object types which were found in Clarke's foreign grave group do not occur in any other burials at Lankhills. All this evidence taken together suggests that Clarke was correct in his proposal that this group of graves was that of travellers from Hungary.

However, we have not yet looked at the bracelets themselves found in these graves. My study concentrates on copper alloy bracelets, and some of those worn by the Lankhills group are of bone and more unusual materials, ivory and iron. Until someone does a large study of the types of bracelets made from other materials found throughout the

Empire, it is impossible to say where these might have originated. However, I can make some statements about the copper alloy bracelets. They are not Pannonian types at all. Instead, types which are commonly found in Britain predominate (**31**) and most of these were certainly made in Britain, for example cogwheel bracelets, whose wholly British distribution was demonstrated in the previous chapter. How can the British bracelets be explained? The evidence seems convincing that the graves are foreign, so why are the skeletons not wearing foreign bracelets?

As I have already mentioned, it might be naive to assume that foreigners will always appear with a full complement of foreign material. Perhaps the custom was only a grave rite, and therefore the women arrived with just the few bracelets they were wearing, and not enough to use in the grave rite (it might be a bit morbid to carry some extra around, so they could be used in the event of your death). Richard Reece suggested another idea to me — perhaps the young girls were born in Britain. If the parents wanted to follow their own culture and give the girls a number of bracelets to wear on the left arm, these would have to be British bracelets rather than Pannonian ones.

Of course, such precise explanations cannot really be proven, and are merely possible accounts which fit the available evidence. However, we can see from this evidence that the links between material culture and identity are not always straightforward. If travellers died quite soon after they reached a certain place, then their dress accessories might be more likely to be a good indication of where they came from, as long as we know enough about the dress customs in other regions to identify a possible source area. If travellers settled in an area for any length of time, however, it is likely that some degree of assimilation would occur. In Britain, Pannonian objects might suggest that the people wearing them had at least passed through Pannonia at some point. Once they arrived in Britain, especially if more than one generation was involved, as time went on, British material would be the only kind available. The British bracelets worn by Clarke's foreign grave group cannot be taken to indicate British origin. The way in which they wore their bracelets in a distinctive row on the left arm might suggest that they still considered themselves to be Pannonian. Conversely, there could be some Pannonians in the cemetery who had chosen not to wear their bracelets in the usual way. Any unusual custom would mark them out to the native population as strangers. It might be the case that sometimes people wanted to try and conceal their origins by conforming with local practices, and even wanted to take on a new identity. It is also likely that after a few generations the travellers would intermarry with locals and perhaps not pass on their culture to future generations. The descendants of these travellers may have regarded themselves as 'British' or as belonging to another local or regional group. Clarke suggests that this can actually be demonstrated at Lankhills by examining the burial ritual in other graves of a later date.

There is an important point to make here. Geographic origin can of course be traced in the genetic makeup of a particular person. However, how the person would be identified genetically and how they would choose to describe themselves might be very different. The objects they deliberately chose to wear to express a certain identity would therefore be a better indicator of how they saw themselves, rather than looking at blood groups or other biological factors. A combination of the two might be especially revealing. An interesting project would be to take a large cemetery where the physical anthropology,

31 Typical British bracelets from the Lankhills cemetery, Winchester. Redrawn after after Griffiths in Clarke 1979

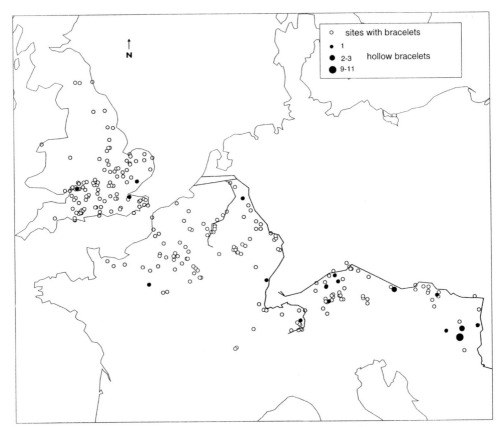

32 Map of hollow bracelets found on sites between the Loire and the Rhine/Danube. Copyright Ellen Swift

the study of the actual skeletal remains, indicates that there are two genetically distinct populations. Then, the grave-goods and personal ornaments associated with each group could be examined. If the material culture present in the graves proved to be identical in both groups, that is, you would not be able to tell that two groups existed from the material record alone, we might initially say that the two groups considered themselves to be the same as each other, and either were not aware of the genetic differences between them or did not consider these to be important. But we would have to remember that they might have signalled their differing identities by using culture which is not archaeologically recoverable, whether objects which have not survived (for example, items made from fragile materials like leather or wood), or non-material culture, such as language, oral traditions of storytelling, dance, and wedding rituals. In the end, it could only be concluded that the two groups shared some aspects of their culture and identity, and that we knew nothing about other aspects.

The more interesting outcome would be if significant differences between the groups could be identified in the material culture deposited in the graves of each group. Then we would be able to suggest that the genetic differences between the two groups had some bearing on how they behaved and what they wore in everyday life — on how they perceived themselves — and that they formed two 'ethnic groups'.

Identity is also just as much about what other people think of *you* as what you think of yourself. Do the people buried at Lankhills stand out more *as* burials than they would perhaps have done in real life? Burial with clothes and other worn dress accessories marks them out from the other burials at Lankhills. However, in real life in late Antiquity, everyone was wearing clothes. The custom of wearing a lot of bracelets on one arm must have been fairly obvious, and the different types of beads and buckles worn may also have been noticeable. (Think about how small a safety pin is, and how in essential respects it is not really much different to most types of earring, but how noticeable safety pins were when first worn as earrings by punks in the 1970s. Assumptions would have immediately have been made about the wearer, though hundreds of years later an archaeologist might not be able to grasp the important symbolic divide between a safety pin and a pearl stud.)

As well as the differences in objects that we can see clearly in the grave and which may or may not have been immediately apparent to their contemporaries, it must be remembered that the jewellery we can recover archaeologically may be just the tip of the iceberg. It could be the case that the clothes worn by the people in the foreign grave group at Lankhills were radically different from the Romano-British norm. Jewellery might merely indicate to us the differences which those living at the time might have seen much more clearly through many varied aspects of dress and lifestyle. Even if the other people buried in the cemetery, the resident population, did not know that the Lankhills foreign group came from Pannonia (or even, perhaps, that such a place existed) they would probably have identified them as strangers and foreigners, whether through their jewellery, clothes, odd burial ritual, or other factors such as language.

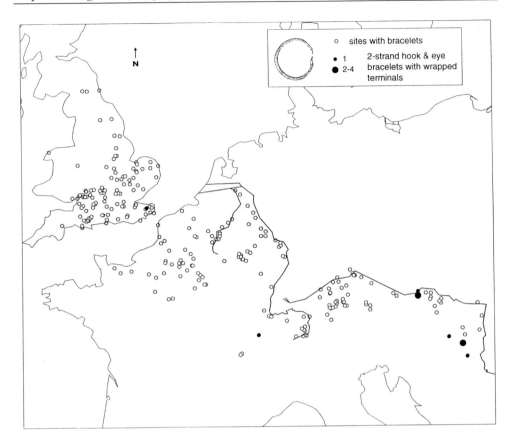

33 Map of two-strand cable bracelets with wrapped terminals found on sites between the Loire and the Rhine/Danube. Copyright Ellen Swift

Chartres

There are also some objects from Pannonia and Sarmatia in northern France. The new excavations of Roman cemeteries in Chartres, as yet unpublished, contain some interesting and unusual material which again is common only in Pannonia/ Sarmatia, and which is similar to that found in the Lankhills burials. Green diamond-faceted beads and flat hexagonal green beads from graves at Chartres suggest an origin beyond the Roman frontier, the flat hexagonal beads having a particular association with Sarmatia, while other graves contain white square cylinder beads and a four-strand cable bracelet with a plain hook and eye fastening which come from Pannonia. However, since these excavations are not yet published, I have been unable to consider any evidence from the grave ritual.

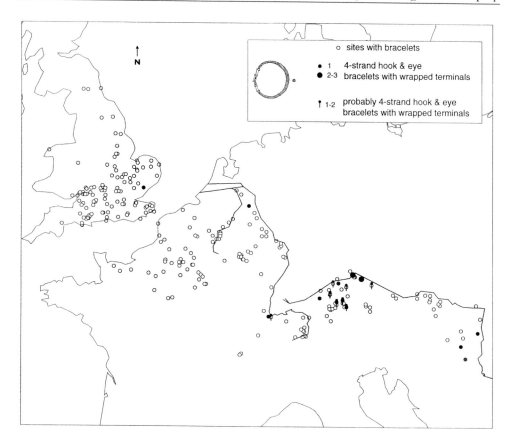

34 Map of four-strand cable bracelets with wrapped terminals found on sites between the Loire and the Rhine/Danube. Copyright Ellen Swift

Krefeld-Gellep

The large mixed Frankish/late Roman cemetery at Krefeld-Gellep in the Upper Rhineland and Roman cemeteries around the important Roman town of Tongeren in Belgium contain several bead and bracelet types which come from the Danube area. The following items appear in graves:

GRAVE 1043 yellow square cylinder beads
GRAVE 3007 four-strand cable bracelet with distinctive terminals, in which a piece of sheet metal is wrapped around each end
GRAVE 3203 fragment of bracelet with wrapped terminals as above
GRAVE 2972 hollow bracelet

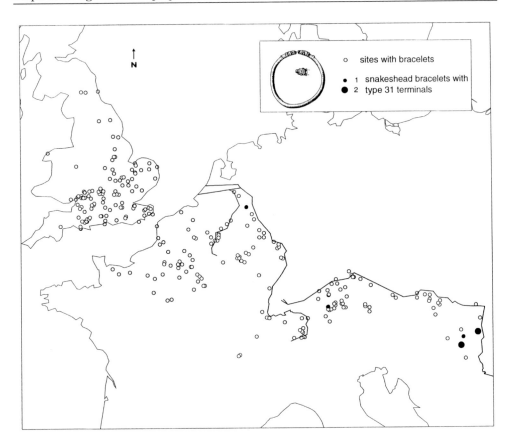

35 Map of snakeshead bracelets type 31 found on sites between the Loire and the Rhine/Danube.
Copyright Ellen Swift

GRAVE 2985 strip bracelet with b13 decoration (scalloped edges, punched dots and a central horizontal groove).
GRAVE 1492 penannular snakeshead bracelet with type 31 terminals (knobbed ends and punched dots).

If we look at the distribution maps for hollow bracelets (**32**), cable bracelets with wrapped terminals (**33-4**) and snakeshead bracelets with type 31 terminals (**35**), a main cluster concentrated in the Danube area contrasts with the presence of a single item at Krefeld-Gellep, a spot far removed from the others. Yellow square cylinder beads (**colour plate 7**) and a strip bracelet with b13 decoration (**36**) are found at Krefeld-Gellep and nearby Tongeren in Belgium, and clustering in the Danube area. It can be suggested that all of these types of object are likely to have originated from the Danube provinces of the Western Roman Empire. Three of the graves at Krefeld Gellep containing objects from the Danube area, 3007, 2972, and 2985, clump together in the west of the cemetery. Grave

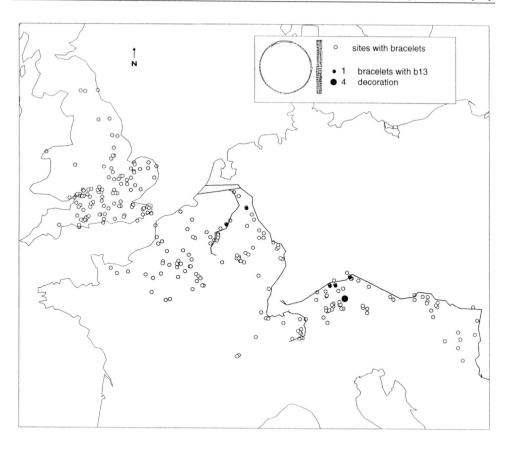

36 Map of bracelets with wavy edges & dots found on sites between the Loire and the Rhine/ Danube. Copyright Ellen Swift

1043 is also in the western part of the cemetery, but further away. The other burials are more widely scattered.

In addition, diamond-faceted green beads in graves 1470 and 2887 may have come from beyond the frontiers, and there are also a number of other very unusual beads at Krefeld Gellep for which I have not been able to find a satisfactory source. According to Nik Cooke, there is also a significant group of glazed vessels from graves in the cemetery, including beakers, amphorae (large storage vessels) and jugs. Glazed pottery is very unusual in the Roman period, apart from in Hungary where glazed jugs in particular are common. Pirling interpreted the glazed vessels at Krefeld-Gellep as being the work of an itinerant Hungarian potter but, considering the new evidence from dress accessories, it now seems likely that they could have been brought to the site by migrants. There is of course also a large Frankish cemetery at Krefeld-Gellep dating to a later period.

Without other evidence such as distinctively different grave ritual, and because only one foreign item occurs in each grave, it is more difficult (compared to the Lankhills

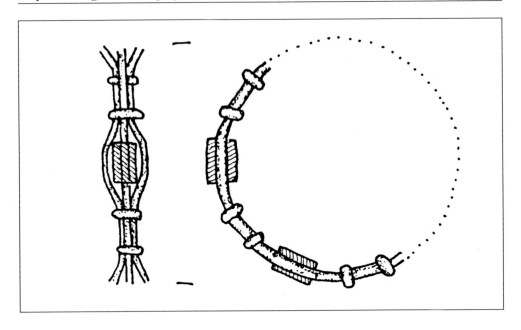

37 Bracelet with threaded glass beads from a cemetery at Tongeren, Belgium. Redrawn after
Vanvinckenroye 1984

burials, for example) to say that the graves in which these items are found are definitely
those of travellers.

It can be said, however, that at one time or another some of the people buried here
had access to the material culture of another region, and the most likely mechanism of
dispersal is that of persons travelling from one area to another and bringing objects with
them. Certainly the presence of six different types of dress accessory which originate
on the Danube (plus Hungarian pottery, and the fact that three of the graves containing
these objects are quite close together), builds up more convincing evidence for a foreign
presence than just one item would do, but it might be risky to assume that the people
buried with one object from the Danube are necessarily the same people who brought the
objects to the site.

Tongeren

At Tongeren, the evidence from grave 37 (from the south-western cemetery excavated by
Vanvinckenroye) is especially striking, as two different items from the Danube area occur
in the same grave. In this grave, the skeleton is wearing a distinctive bracelet made of
strands of wire with threaded glass beads (**37**). These bracelets are otherwise found in the
Danube area (**38**), and have a specific type of wrapped fastening which also occurs on cable
bracelets characteristic of the Danube provinces, as already demonstrated above (**33-4**).
The skeleton is also wearing a bead necklace containing long blue hexagonal cylinder

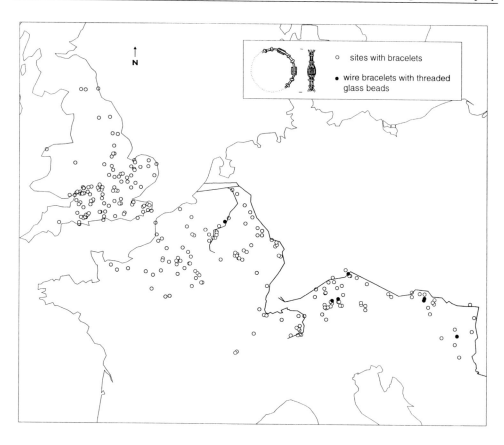

*38 Map of bracelets with threaded glass beads found on sites between the Loire and the Rhine/
Danube.* Copyright Ellen Swift

beads which are found in the same region, mainly on the line of the Danube river itself
(**colour plate 8**).

Other evidence from Tongeren already mentioned above, though not from specific
grave contexts, includes yellow square cylinder beads (**colour plate 7**) and strip bracelets
with scalloped edges and punched dots as found at Krefeld-Gellep (**36**). As shown
previously, these items are found exclusively in the Danube region, apart from their
occurrence at these two sites.

Most of the burials discussed here are on military sites (e.g. Krefeld-Gellep, a military
graveyard) or the graves themselves contain military material such as crossbow brooches
(e.g. Lankhills). The easiest explanation for the presence of material from the eastern part
of the study area in the more westerly provinces of the Roman Empire is that the people
responsible for bringing it travelled west with the army. This does not preclude women
travelling, since we know that many women accompanied the army. It is interesting that
there seems to be more evidence of a movement east to west than vice versa. However we

have to consider quite carefully why this might be the case. In part, it is because material travelling east to west is easier to identify archaeologically. There is quite a large quantity of material dating to the late Roman period published in site reports from the Danube provinces, which meant that I could be confident about identifying objects which come from this area. Distribution maps of the object types found on these sites show large clusters in the Danube area and fewer or no objects elsewhere. Areas such as Belgica, however, have fewer published sites. Object types which are found on sites in this area may only occur in one or two published site reports or museum collections. They are not known about in sufficient numbers to be confident that they are regional and produced only in Belgica. Since we cannot be sure they were made in Belgica, where they occur elsewhere they cannot be used as evidence of movement.

However, it might be thought that, with the wide range of bracelet types specific to Britannia, movement of people who lived in Britain to areas further east would be relatively simple to trace. There are several Continental sites where British types of bracelets have been found, for example, Augst in Switzerland, where eight bracelets can be positively identified as British types (**39-40**), and two of these occur in the same grave. Does this mean that some people once travelled from Britain to Switzerland in the late Roman period, and that they were buried at Augst? Or does it mean that a British craftsperson moved to Augst and started making bracelets there? The presence of several foreigners is much more convincing if it can be identified through several different object types. Otherwise, it could just be the craftsperson who has moved (who is of course still foreign), and begun to produce goods in a different area. At the moment there are no bead types which can be identified as 'British' so it is no good looking for these at Augst. There *is* a type of belt set which was definitely made in Britain. *If* it occurred outside Britain, in combination with other evidence, this might suggest the presence of Romano-British travellers. However, this belt set type does not occur at all in the area of the Continent under study.

The combined evidence from objects which have travelled far from where they were made does enable us to suggest that there may have been quite a few people moving from the Danube area of the Roman Empire to regions further west in the late Roman period. There may have been movement west to east as well, but it is harder to spot.

'Barbarians' within the Empire

Can we find any evidence for barbarian incursions into the Roman Empire? Some material, objects from Sarmatia and other areas beyond the frontier, has already been discussed. This type of investigation is fraught with difficulties, not least that the various barbarian groups — Goths, Visigoths, Vandals, etc. — were of course only named by their Roman observers and may not have thought of themselves as unified 'tribes' or ethnic or cultural groups. It might be assumed that looking for 'barbarian' objects would be easier than spotting provincial Roman objects which have moved from one province or region of the Western Roman Empire to another. Germanic culture is more obviously distinct from Roman material, and therefore will stand out more. Germanic people wore

39 British type bracelet found at Augst.
Redrawn after Riha 1990

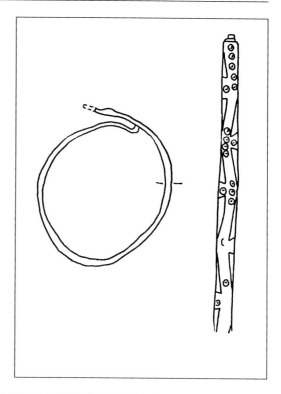

40 British type bracelet found at Augst. Redrawn after Riha 1990

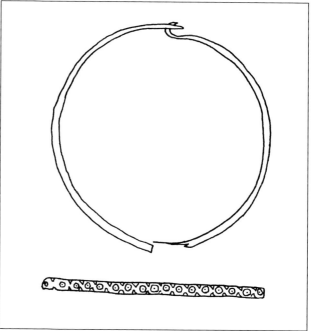

completely different types of brooches. Their visibly distinct dress custom can be clearly seen in early medieval cemeteries. It might be thought that this custom would be readily identifiable. However, the main problem here is that in the Germanic homelands beyond the frontiers cremation was a popular burial practice. Unfortunately this has the effect of destroying much evidence about Germanic customs and material contemporary with (but outside) the Roman Empire, which is necessary for any comparison with supposedly Germanic material within the frontier. Furthermore, James suggests in his study of early medieval south-western France that Germanic people are very difficult to find because they assimilate and quickly adopt the same burial rite as the native Gallo-Romans — effectively *becoming* Gallo-Romans — a disjunction between biological and cultural identity of the type already mentioned above.

Foreigners in western France

A number of sites within the frontier have unusual material which has been associated with the possible presence of 'barbarians'. There is some interesting evidence from very late cemeteries. For example, archaeologists working in Normandy are beginning to link together a number of different strands of evidence for the presence of strangers in this area in the early fifth century, when the far West of Gaul was still ostensibly under Roman control, but when the barbarians were starting to establish separate kingdoms or hegemonies in other areas.

The archaeologists working on the late Roman and medieval cemetery at Fontenay, near Caen, carried out a full study of the skeletons buried there. They found that up to 20% of the fifth-century burials at Fontenay formed a distinctive group when the physical anthropology was taken into account, that is when the bones of the skeleton were examined, particularly the skull. The skulls in these burials had been intentionally deformed. They were flattened and elongated, probably by wrapping the head when the child was still young with crosswise bandages (**41**). This custom has been associated with the Huns, a tribe of barbarians notorious for their invasion of the Roman Empire in the early fifth century. Head flattening was certainly quite a widespread practice in the area around the Black Sea, where the Huns are thought to have come from, and dates back to the Neolithic. It may be associated with many of the peoples who are listed by the Romans as 'barbarian invaders'.

Some of the graves with deformed skulls contained very unusual objects. Grave 300, for example, contained two odd brooches (**colour plate 14**). The brooches have a large semicircular plate at the lower end, balanced by a tapering foot. The plate is sometimes decorated with polished garnets and sometimes with other cast geometric patterns. These brooches were found in pairs in several graves, and were worn in pairs on the shoulders, in the style which we have already associated with tribes living beyond the frontiers in free Germany. Brooches of this type have been found in several cemeteries in western France (the modern administrative region of Calvados). However, they are by no means a usual part of the material culture of this area. Examining fifth-century burial sites in Hungary (which had been overrun by barbarians at the end of the fourth century, and was by this time no longer under Roman jurisdiction), personal ornaments frequently occur in the graves, characteristically including garnet-set buckles and brooches of the type described

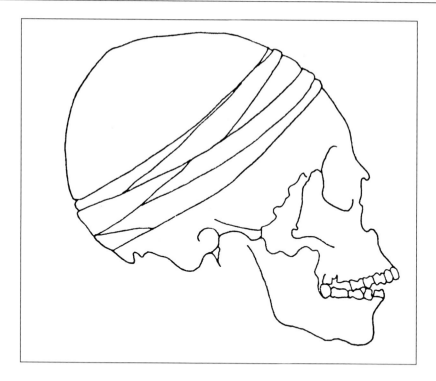

41 Diagram of how bandages can be wound around a skull to alter its shape, a practice common in the Black sea region. Redrawn after Musée de Normandie 198x

above (**colour plate 15**). Silver earrings in a crescent shape, worn by men rather than women, are also found at Fontenay. In the Roman period earrings were worn by women only, and this shape is not known. This additional evidence of non-'Roman' practices and material culture at Fontenay has also been linked to the Asiatic steppe.

It is known from documentary sources that Attilla and his horsemen swept through the Empire in the early fifth century AD, supposedly leaving behind such a trail of devastation that their name became notorious (and was re-used comparatively recently to refer to invaders such as the Germans, for example). Their course led through Gaul to North Italy. It is also known that the Romans used Hunnic mercenary soldiers in Gaul to suppress other, Germanic barbarians. The Huns were a collection of nomadic peoples with a distinctively different culture to the settled peoples of the Roman Empire. A scholar travelling on the steppe in the early part of this century, Peisker, recorded customs and material culture among the nomadic tribes, and was obviously struck by their resemblance to customs noted by contemporary Roman observers of the Hunnic invasions. These included circular migrations over hundreds of miles, and more specific customs such as using cooking utensils of iron and bronze, particularly cauldrons, and the practice of placing meat under the saddle. Late antique sources call this the barbarian method for cooking meat, but Peisker says that it was to prevent saddle sores.

Could the burials at Fontenay be those of Huns? The seductive image of Attilla and his hordes is dangerous; even if we can identify strange objects and practices which have an association with the Black Sea region, this does not necessarily mean they are of Hunnic origin. Metal saddle fittings and cauldrons are particularly associated with the Huns, and form part of a distinctive nomadic material culture. These objects do not occur at Fontenay. The other evidence so far amassed, including both foreign objects and foreign customs of dress and body malformation, suggests merely that there were people present who originally came from the Black Sea area. They may easily have belonged to one of many tribes who are known to have been travelling in this region during the fourth and fifth centuries. It is easier to spot anomalous burial practices and material than it is to make a definite association with a historically named people, who may not have had a single culture anyway, nor existed as a distinct cultural group. The archaeologists reporting on the site present the evidence and leave the question open.

However, the evidence for strangers at Fontenay is certainly striking, in terms of both unusual material culture which can be linked to the Black Sea area, the way in which this material was worn, and other practices such as deliberate cranial deformation. We can only imagine how the native population may have reacted to men wearing earrings, and women with strange jewellery and deformed heads (interestingly enough often given to aliens in modern popular culture). The combined evidence is strong enough to suggest that we have found some barbarians here, who would have been marked out through dress and general appearance from the local population, though of course we are drifting away from the fourth century and into the post-Roman west. Incidentally, the practice of head flattening gradually dies out in this cemetery. In the fifth century, ten to twenty percent of the burials are of people using this custom; in the sixth this has dropped to five to ten percent, and it is no longer found by the seventh century.

Objects travelling between the Roman Empire and areas beyond the frontiers

It is interesting to examine the types of material which are found within the Roman Empire and which also occur beyond the frontiers. In some cases the objects seem to have travelled one way, in some another, and in some they may not have travelled at all but been produced locally in the two areas.

Late Roman bead and bracelet types are not generally found beyond the Roman frontier, with the exceptions of some kinds of beads, such as blue diamond-faceted beads, and annular beads with trail decoration. These are a special case, and will be examined in more detail later on. Although both crossbow brooches and belt fittings do occur outside the Roman Empire, there is a marked difference between the distribution patterns of these two types of object in areas not ruled by Rome. Crossbow brooches only make it beyond the frontier in very small quantities, whereas buckles and belt fittings are much more frequent finds in free Germany, with noticeable concentrations in various areas. This could be time-linked; the buckles and belt fittings which are found in free Germany have later dates, often drifting into the fifth century, when it is known that there was far greater movement between the two areas. The small number of crossbow brooches which

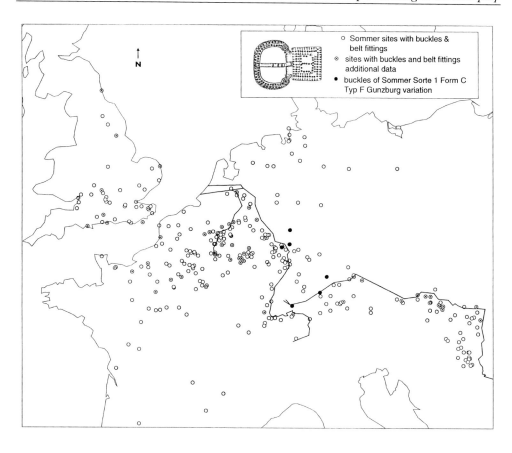

42 Map of Sommer's 'Gunzburg variation' buckles, imitating late Roman material and found just beyond and around the frontier. Copyright Ellen Swift

are found on the wrong side of the frontier have dates which span the fourth century. If anything their stylistic dates tend to be earlier in the fourth century rather than later.

All crossbow brooches, and most belt sets, which do cross the frontier can be confidently identified as Roman. They were made in provincial Roman workshops within the Empire. Small differences in decorative technique allowed Sommer to distinguish between buckles and belt fittings which had been made in free Germany in imitation of the Roman model, and those which had been made within the Empire but had travelled outside it. The imitations which Sommer identified are found in a small region just around the frontier in southern Germany (**42**) while 'genuine' Roman material has a different distribution, with a fairly high proportion of material occurring around the North sea coast, particularly the mouth of the Elbe. The buckles and belt fittings which occur beyond the frontier also cluster within the Empire around the line of the river Meuse, (Belgium/northern France) in the row of new fortified settlements established in the early fifth century (**colour plate 16**). It is much disputed who exactly occupied these military fortifications. As well as the link with the North Sea coast, suggested by the buckles that are found in both places (and which originated within the Empire) there are also some objects at these sites which are mainly found in free Germany, as established by Böhme.

Böhme studied 'Germanic' grave goods between two rivers, the Elbe, in north Germany (and quite a way beyond the Roman Rhine frontier), and the Loire. He classified a number of distinctive Germanic brooch types, which were worn by women in pairs on each shoulder, to pin a tunic (**43**). This was a pan-European custom before the Roman conquest, but had died out within the Roman Empire by the fourth century, though it did linger on in some areas under Roman rule until the third century. Böhme interpreted the appearance of some of these brooch types within the Roman Empire, for example at sites along the Meuse, as evidence for the presence of Germanic people. So-called 'tutulus' brooches (from the German, meaning 'cone-shaped') are one example, a very odd and to the modern eye hideously ugly type of brooch. They were worn by women in pairs, and resemble two inverted cones sticking out from the shoulders. These tutulus brooches are usually worn at burial in pairs where they occur in graves in northern France and Belgium (**44**), and, as mentioned previously, it is not the usual Roman practice to be buried wearing clothes and other accessories.

The male skeletons found at the same sites were also dressed at burial, and are provided with their weapons. Sometimes Roman objects such as buckles and belt fittings appear in the graves (**45**). This appears to be a manifestation of the 'military' Roman burial rite identified by Nik Cooke, already discussed in chapter two. These link through material and dress customs with free Germany, and evident differences from normal provincial Roman burial practices in the female graves, together with the Roman military appearance of the male graves, have been used to suggest that the people buried at these sites were Germanic troops recruited into the Roman army, who had brought their families with them. They could, possibly, be members of those Germanic tribes settled within the Empire who had been given land in this area in exchange for military service.

It has been argued by Halsall that the people buried in these graves might not be Germanic at all. Occupants of the graves are buried wearing clothes, which is not normal Roman practice. However it is not normal Germanic practice either. Cremation would be the usual Germanic rite. The tutulus brooches also have minor features which show that they are not exactly the same as the ones which occur beyond the frontier. They may well have been copies of Germanic material actually produced by workshops within the frontiers. Halsall suggested that the popularity of Germanic fashion alone could account for their presence, and that they need not signify ethnically Germanic women. The rich provision of these graves has been used to suggest that the unusual grave custom is linked to a display of wealth and status rather than being related to an ethnic practice. The male graves in particular do not have any objects that are more common beyond the frontiers than inside the Empire.

However, it is difficult to explain away the links via artefacts to free Germany through fashion alone. Why do belt sets of various types occur in these burials and in a significant minority in free Germany? If tutulus brooches were a general late Roman fashion, why are they not more widespread? Why are they still worn in the Germanic dress style? Why do

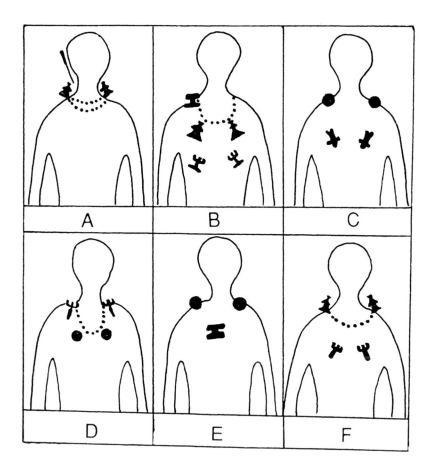

43 *Germanic/Celtic female dress fashion, here shown by the placement of jewellery in fifth-century female graves at various sites in northern France, Belgium and Germany: A Cortrat, B Vermand, C Krefeld-Gellep, D Mahndorf, E Sahlenburg, F Vert-la-Gravelle. A brooch was worn on each shoulder to pin the tunic, often with a string of beads suspended between the two.* Redrawn after Böhme 1974

they often occur with other unusual 'non-Roman' objects, such as amber beads (found, for example, in a grave with tutulus brooches at Cortrat in France)? There is a danger that, in the recent efforts of archaeologists to re-examine common assumptions, and to question accounts based on a simplistic reading of the material evidence, explanations are rejected which may still remain likely. The suggestion that these are the graves of Germanic soldiers and/or settlers is certainly as plausible as any alternative ideas, which themselves fail to account completely for the patterns found in the material. There is no reason why the graves of Germanic people settled within the Empire, especially after a few generations, need be identical to those of their forbears in the homelands. It is likely that as soon as people settle in an area remote from their original homeland there is some cultural

44 *Tutulus brooches from a grave at Saint Vigor-le-Grand, Pouligny, which would have been worn in a pair, one on each shoulder.* Copyright P. David, Musée de Normandie

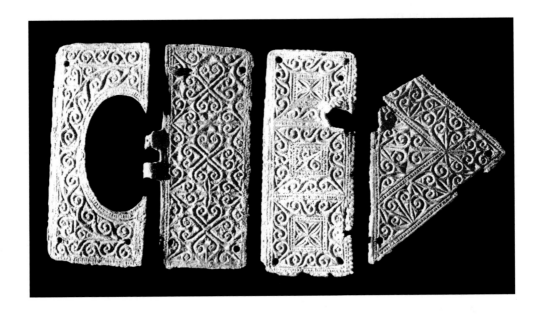

45 *Elaborate chip carved belt set from Saint Vigor-le-Grand, Pouligny.* Copyright P. David, Musée de Normandie

drift in practices which results from their interaction with the local population and their separation from the homeland. This may result in either an exaggerated differentiation from the local population, or gradual assimilation within it. Those living in the new area may even stick more closely to their cultural practices than the original population living in the homelands. For example, most Israelis are far more secular than Jewish minorities living in other countries.

Whatever the identity of the people buried with this new grave rite (and if they are not Germanic, links with the North Sea coast area of free Germany still remain to be explained), they were certainly influential, as the rite spread in later centuries to become the norm.

Gold and silver objects

As mentioned above, a type of late Roman brooch, the crossbow brooch, worn by military/ civilian officials, is also sometimes found beyond the Roman frontier. In this case, however, the factors which affect their distribution seem to be rather different. Outside the Empire, dispersed in a wide variety of locations, and often occurring as single finds. They show no particular concentration in one area. A disproportionate number are made of gold or silver (**colour plate 17**). I collected information on over 1000 brooches from within the western Empire. Of these, only seven were gold. Three of the gold brooches were from the west of Britain; three were from Trier in the Rhineland of Germany. This is as we might expect, since Trier was the residence of the western Emperor for some of the fourth century, and there must have been many other high-status officials in Trier during his period of occupation. The remaining brooch was from Childeric's grave in Tournai, Belgium, which strictly speaking does not count, as by the time Childeric was buried this area was not within the Empire per se but had been ceded to the Germanic Franks, Childeric being their king. Now, considering evidence from beyond the frontiers, of the ten brooches I came across, four were gold. Although it is difficult to be sure (as the numbers are so small, and as I have not done a systematic search for brooches outside the Empire in the same detail as that carried out within), it seems that gold brooches travel beyond the frontier more readily than brooches in other materials.

It seems likely that crossbow brooches which travel beyond the frontiers may have been carried to their final resting place by people who were not the original wearers. For the most part they do not occur in grave contexts, but as stray finds or part of hoards of material. It appears to be the case that, while crossbow brooches in other materials — for example copper alloy — had no particular value or significance outside their normal milieu, gold brooches *would* be valued. We might suggest from this that the barbarians living outside the Empire were not interested in symbols of Roman culture and authority — the crossbow brooch as a symbol in itself — but in the intrinsic value of the precious metal. One of the sites beyond the frontier where a crossbow is found, Lengerich in Germany, also produced a hoard of late Roman precious metal, which tends to support this idea. The presence of objects beyond the frontiers can therefore be seen to have as much to do with the value of the specific objects in this particular region as it does anything else. It does not appear to be related to the movement of people who might have originally owned the objects (in this case, presumably high-status officials in the

Roman Empire, who, we would assume, would not be at all likely to want to travel deep into enemy territory). These patterns, which may be present merely because the objects have an intrinsic value which copper alloy objects would not have had, suggest that it may be dangerous to assume too much about the original wearers from the distributions of precious metal objects in general. From this example, it seems that gold and silver objects are more likely than copper alloy objects to be deposited in secondary contexts that do not reflect their original use.

Opaque beads with trail decoration

When examining various types of artefact which occur on both sides of the Roman frontiers, it is sometimes very difficult to decide where the object originally came from, and if this is the same as where they were buried, lost, or otherwise became part of the archaeological record. We must be careful to consider other likely events, such as production in more than one place, or the production centre moving around through time. A good case study is the evidence relating to a new type of glass bead which appears within the Roman Empire at the end of the fourth century and the beginning of the fifth (**colour plate 18**). These beads are unlike the preferred type in the mid-fourth century and earlier, small, discreet, translucent beads of one colour in simple geometric shapes. They are larger than typical Roman beads and most often ring-shaped (often called annular). This shape results from an enlarged perforation through the bead. Less frequently, they may be cylindrical, cone-shaped, bun-shaped, or jug-shaped. All these types also have a wide perforation. The beads are made from opaque glass, often black. They are decorated with a thread or trail of molten glass that is applied after the bead has been made, and consequently, this trail is raised above the surface of the bead. The trail may be in one or several colours, or it may be of white glass. There is a range of common motifs, no doubt based on the practicalities of the technique — the trail must be quite difficult to apply. The most ambitious one I have come across, a bead supposedly decorated with human faces, is not especially successful; it takes a vivid imagination to pick out the eyes, nose and mouth. The beads are usually decorated more simply. There may be a wavy line around the bead, or it may be decorated with several superimposed circles, which form 'eyes'.

Opaque beads with trail decoration, though with no precursors in the Roman Empire, are quite similar to the beads which were worn pre-conquest. These were often highly decorated and colourful.

We are quite lucky in that we know where some of the beads with trail decoration were manufactured. Excavations at Trier in the Rhineland of Germany in the early part of this century uncovered evidence of a glass workshop for the production of this type of bead — a crucible with molten remains, glass offcuts, and numerous opaque beads with trail decoration. The Rhineland was the main production area for late Roman glass, but this is the only site where evidence exists specifically for the production of beads. Opaque beads with a wavy trail have also been commonly found on other sites in and around Trier, which was also a production centre for glass vessels. The site of the bead workshop was dated by the excavator to the late fourth century.

Schulze looked at several specific types of these beads, decorated with bands around

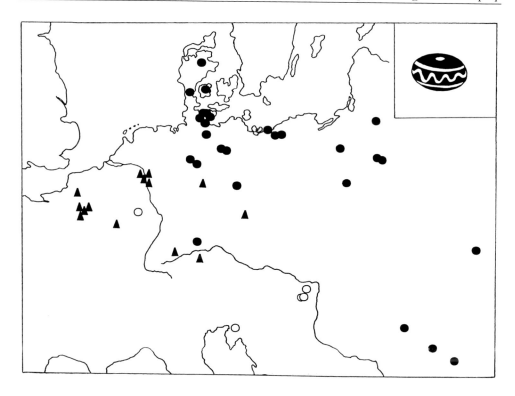

46 Distribution map of annular beads with coloured bands and wavy trails. Circles indicate fourth-century finds, triangles those from the fifth century. Redrawn after Schulze 1978

the circumference, and wavy trails. She found that in the fourth century they were distributed mostly outside the Roman Empire, in free Germany. By the fifth century they are found in increasing quantities inside the former Empire, particularly in northern France and the lower Rhine (**46**). From this evidence she suggested that, since the position of a fourth-century workshop was known at Trier, in the fourth century the Romans were exporting these beads to the Germanic tribes living beyond the frontier. When the Empire collapsed and there was a large migration of people from free Germany, Germanic people moved within the former Empire bringing the beads with them. This is a plausible idea based on the evidence available at the time, but it may also owe something to more recent colonial history, in which beads were used in Africa as gifts or as a medium of exchange. It is obviously tempting to make a parallel between this and the situation in the fourth century. However with new evidence collected by myself from sites which have been excavated over the last few years, and with the evidence from a new publication by Tempelmann-Macyzynska on the beads found beyond the frontiers throughout the Roman period, this interpretation must be reassessed. It seems clear now that the wavy trail beads discussed by Schulze which are found beyond the frontiers cannot possibly be exported from a manufacturing centre within the Empire at Trier. There are far too many, many more than have in fact been found at and around Trier. Even more telling,

95

they occur beyond the frontiers in the second and third centuries as well as the fourth, so they cannot all have been produced in a fourth-century workshop. Given that at all the new sites which have been excavated in the last few years, beads of this type are found in contexts with dates at the end of the fourth and edging into the fifth century, it would not be too surprising if the workshop at Trier turned out to be a bit later than previously supposed. The site report was written in 1925, when sites with any surviving Roman material would have been automatically dated to the fourth century.

Combining all the evidence, wavy trail beads of second-, third- and fourth-century date occur predominantly outside the Roman Empire. They begin to appear within the Empire in the fourth, especially late fourth, and fifth centuries onwards. If the workshop at Trier does have a late date, in the very late fourth century, or at the turn of the fifth century, it would therefore cater to the demand at this date for the beads within the Empire, rather than in free Germany.

It may be too simplistic to assume that these beads represent the presence of Germanic people rather than the indigenous population of the Roman Empire. They are found on many different types of Roman site, particularly those of late date. Unlike tutulus brooches, they do not occur in association with other 'Germanic' material any more often than they are found with common Roman items, and seem to have been worn fairly indiscriminately by the local population, which may by this date have included some Germanic peoples. While 'Roman' styles of bead die out in the fifth century, wavy trail beads and diamond-faceted beads (which were also worn for centuries beyond the frontiers before they appeared within the Roman Empire) continued to be worn for several centuries in some areas.

The archaeological evidence from this chapter therefore supports the historical sources in their assertion that this period was a time of substantial migration and movement in the late Roman world. From the archaeological evidence, much of this movement appears to have been connected with the Roman army, rather than with the supposed 'barbarian invasions'. In the most clear-cut example, at Fontenay, we can see people who do appear to be barbarians, marked out through their distinctive dress and other cultural practices. There is also convincing evidence from Lankhills of long-distance travel from the eastern end of the Western Empire.

However, the evidence also shows that the divide between stranger and native, between Roman and barbarian, was not unbridgeable. We know that Germanic people were fighting in the Roman army. Are they Roman or Germanic? This confusion of identity which must have been felt by many in real life is mirrored in the archaeological record. Some objects which were once found only beyond the frontiers now occur within the Empire as well, but have become so widespread that they may have become Roman fashions in their own right. Other objects and dress customs are the subject of heated debate. The ambiguous nature of skeletons buried with grave goods and dress accessories is perhaps inevitable. Wherever people move from one place to another, the interaction of different cultures over a period of time results in the transformation of both.

Essentially, what matters is not an abstract definition as 'Roman' or 'Germanic' but an understanding of the complexity of different identities in the late Roman West. The material evidence shows us that, on the cusp of its breakdown, the late Roman Western

Empire was a melting pot of many different cultures and practices, interacting on a daily basis at all levels of society. Far from the Roman army keeping the barbarians out, the Roman practice of Germanic recruitment and the settlement of Germanic soldiers within the Empire in exchange for service may have had a greater impact on the late Roman West than the more obviously hostile Germanic tribes attacking the frontier itself. However, the defence of the frontier undoubtedly has its own importance in any account of the late Roman West, and forms the subject of the penultimate chapter.

1 Hand-coloured and gilded illustration of Roman metalwork from a German antiquarian
volume, 'Der Altertümer unserer Heidnischen Vorzeit' (Antiquities of our Pagan Prehistory) by
L. Lindenschmidt, Volume 3 (1881) Heft IX taf 4. Copyright Society of Antiquaries of
London

2 *Hand-coloured illustration of glass beads of the medieval period from a German antiquarian volume, 'Der Altertümer unserer Heidnischen Vorzeit' (Antiquities of our Pagan Prehistory) by L. Lindenschmidt, Volume 4 (1900) Taf.22.* Copyright Society of Antiquaries of London

3   *Hand-coloured illustration of Roman pottery from a German antiquarian volume, 'Der Altertümer unserer Heidnischen Vorzeit' (Antiquities of our Pagan Prehistory) by L. Lindenschmidt, Volume 4 (1900) Band III Taf. 4.* Copyright Society of Antiquaries of London

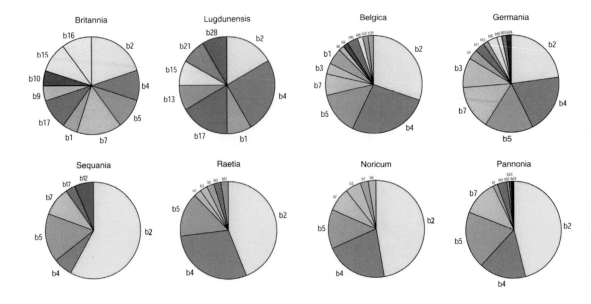

4 *Pie charts showing proportions of the different foot patterns on crossbow brooches occurring in each provincial area.* Copyright Ellen Swift

5 *Late Roman belt buckle and buckle plate from Sees, France, with stylised animal ornament.* Copyright P. David, Musée de Normandie

6   *Late Roman necklaces and bracelets of glass beads from Bregenz, illustrating a range of different types, including blue heart-shaped beads (1) yellow biconical beads (7), and long blue biconical beads (6).* Copyright Vorarlberger Landesmusem, Bregenz

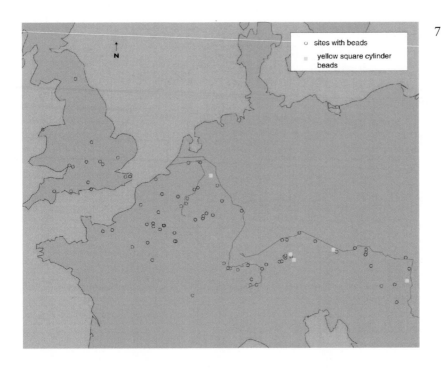

7 *Map showing the distribution of yellow square cylinder beads between the Loire and the Rhine/ Danube.* Copyright Ellen Swift

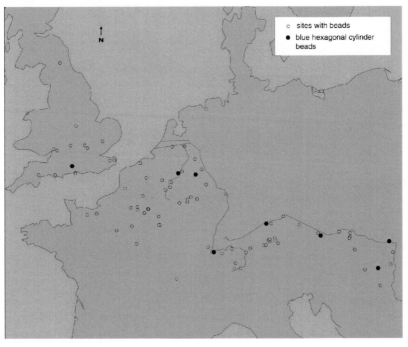

8 *Map showing the distribution of blue hexagonal cylinder beads between the Loire and the Rhine/ Danube.* Copyright Ellen Swift

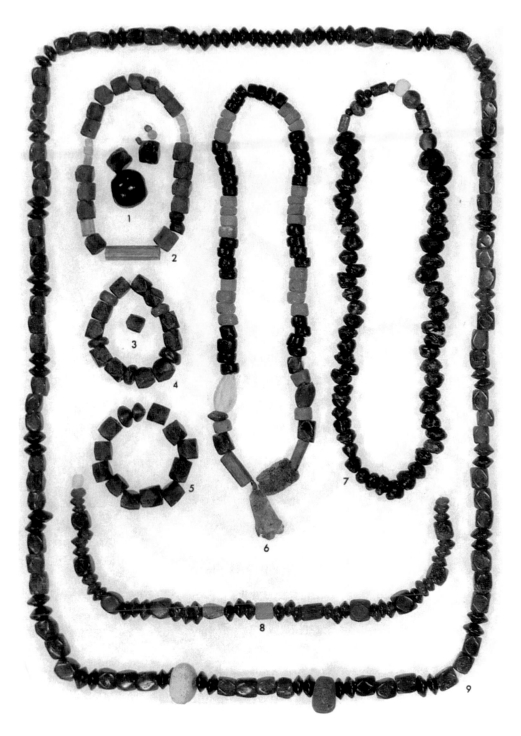

9 *Late Roman necklaces and bracelets of glass beads from Bregenz, containing among others blue diamond faceted beads and long green hexagonal cylinder beads.* Copyright Vorarlberger Landesmusem, Bregenz

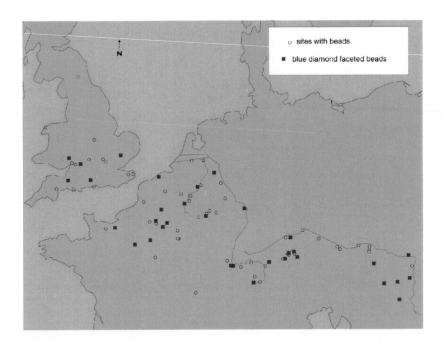

10 *Map showing the distribution of blue diamond faceted beads between the Loire and the Rhine/ Danube.* Copyright Ellen Swift

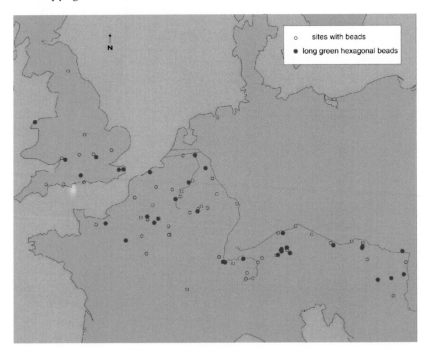

11 *Map showing the distribution of green hexagonal cylinder beads between the Loire and the Rhine/Danube.* Copyright Ellen Swift

12 *Pit burial of a family group with worn personal ornaments from Stour Street, Canterbury.* Copyright Canterbury Archaeological Trust

13 *Detail from the Stour Street pit burial, showing a pile of bracelets encircling the wrist bones of a skeleton.* Copyright Canterbury Archaeological Trust

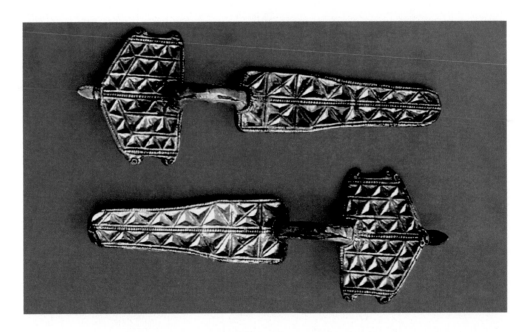

14 *Pair of brooches with flat near-semicircular heads from a grave at the late Roman and early medieval cemetery of Fontenay, Normandy, France.* Copyright P. David, Musée de Normandie

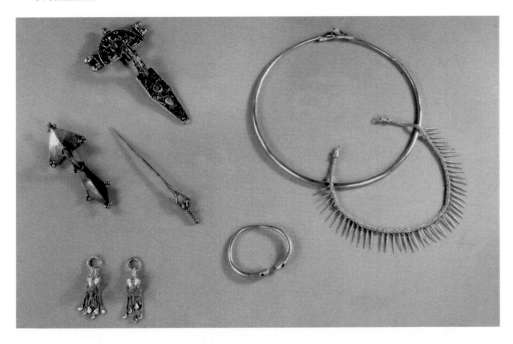

15 *Grave group of gold and silver jewellery from Untersiebenbrunn, in the Austria/Hungary border region, including brooches with semicircular heads, and a fringed necklace characteristic of the Black Sea region.* Copyright Kunsthistorisches Museum, Vienna

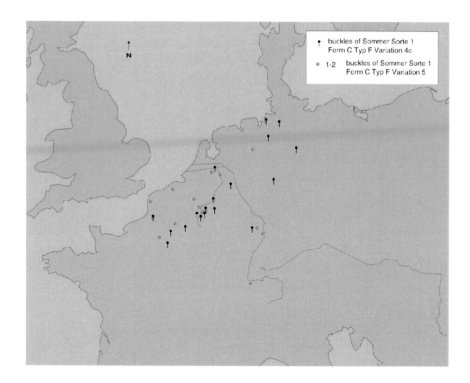

16 Map showing the distribution of two different buckle types (Sorte 1 Form C Typ F Var 4a & 5) in the lower Rhine/Meuse area. Copyright Ellen Swift

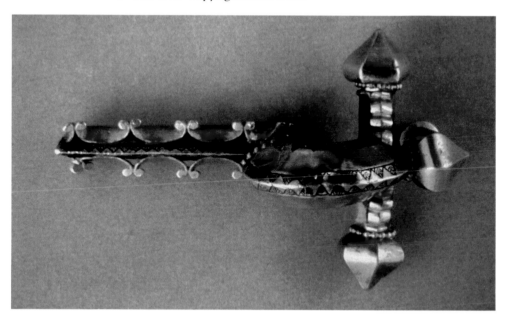

17 The gold type 6ii crossbow brooch found in the Moray Firth, Scotland. Copyright British Museum

18 Roman glass beads from Bregenz: the melon beads (6) are from the early Roman period. Opaque beads with trail decoration, of fourth-fifth-century date, include beads with 'eyes' (4,7,8), swags (7, 10), coloured bands (12,13) and feather trails (9). Copyright Vorarlberger Landesmusem, Bregenz

Fibulæ aureæ et gemmatæ.

19 *Page from the original illustrations of Childeric's grave goods, made in 1655, from 'Anastasis Childerici I' by Chiflet. The gold 'Kolbenarmringe' is the central illustration.* Copyright Romische-Germanisch Zentralmuseum Mainz

20 Christ before Pilate, the sixth-century mosiac in the church of St. Apollinaire Nuovo, Ravenna. Pilate appears to be wearing a crossbow brooch on his right shoulder. Copyright Longo Editore

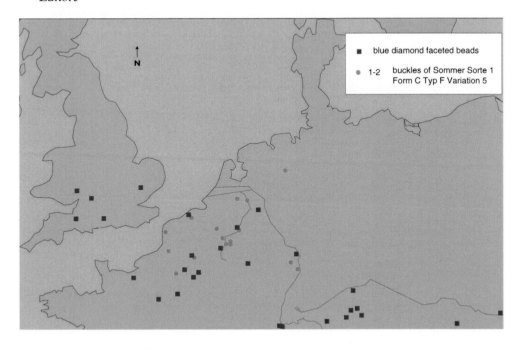

21 Map showing the contrasting distributions of blue diamond faceted beads and buckles of Sorte 1 Form C Typ Variation 5 in the lower Rhine/Meuse area. Copyright Ellen Swift

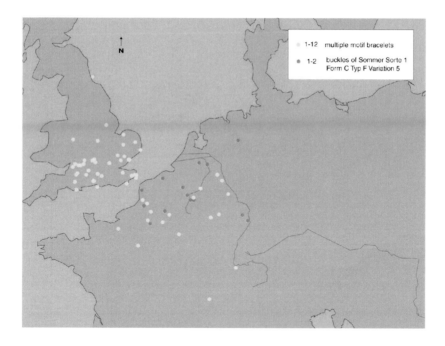

22 Map showing the contrasting distributions of multiple motif bracelets and buckles of Sorte 1 Form C Typ Variation 5 in the lower Rhine/Meuse area. Copyright Ellen Swift

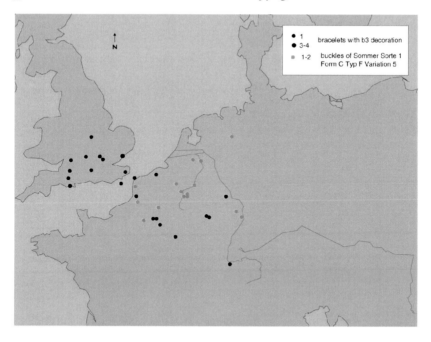

23 Map showing the contrasting distributions of bracelets with a line of punched dots separated by pairs of notches, and buckles of Sorte 1 Form C Typ Variation 5 in the lower Rhine/Meuse area. Copyright Ellen Swift

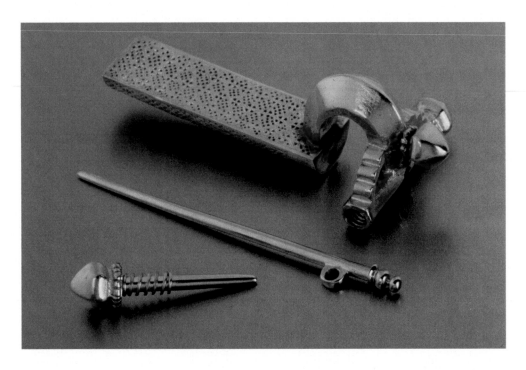

24 Replica of the type 7 gold crossbow brooch with opus interrasile *(openwork) foot decoration found in the grave of Childeric, King of the Franks.* Copyright Römsiche-Germanisch Zentralmuseum Mainz

25 Roman gold solidus now in the Ashmolean Museum, Oxford. Solidii like this one were melted down to produce Germanic 'Kolbenarmringe'. Copyright Richard Reece & Ashmolean Museum, Oxford

4   Army movements and the collapse of the frontiers

The frontier is a key area of interest for those studying the late Roman West and the breakdown of Roman authority. Looking at the occurrence of objects on sites along the frontier is one way of studying frontier activity. Objects such as crossbow brooches and belt sets formed part of a uniform. Some of the time, they represent soldiers in the archaeological record. We might be able to use these objects to look at the movement of the army in the final period of Roman occupation in the Western Empire. Types of crossbow brooch and belt set popular at different times could represent the presence of soldiers in various places at one time or another. Moreover, civilian objects sometimes have a military distribution, and these can add to the picture.

Cross-channel forts

In chapter two, I showed that a very wide survey of evidence from a large area of the Western Empire has established which decorative styles of objects were popular in different places. We have seen in the last chapter that it is sometimes possible to isolate unusual material found in graves and to use this in combination with other evidence to suggest that the occupants of the graves, or others at the site, may have travelled from another area. Quite unexpectedly, civilian objects — bracelets — can be used to trace contacts between two specific military sites in the late Roman West. The sites are Oudenburg, a fort on the channel coast in modern-day Belgium, and Portchester Castle, on the other side of the channel in Hampshire. Both were occupied by soldiers in the late fourth century and Oudenburg in particular has a very large and well-furnished late Roman cemetery.

At Oudenburg, several of the graves contained unusual bracelets. Two of these graves are quite near to each other in the cemetery, in the same row. The other graves are further away and wide apart. Grave 78 contained three interesting bracelets. Firstly, a distinctive cogwheel bracelet, so called because of its characteristic toothed edges (**24**). The example at Oudenburg is the only cogwheel bracelet which I have found on the Continent, after examining bracelets from hundreds of Continental sites. Cogwheel bracelets are otherwise found only in Britain, and are extremely widespread and popular throughout the fourth century, as we can see from the map (**25**). The next unusual bracelet in this grave was a moulded penannular bracelet with a circle and dot stamp at the terminals (**47**), again, a type which occurs predominantly in Britain (**48**) . (Sometimes bracelets with this type of terminal (type 1) are decorated with the multiple motif pattern which was used only by British workshops.) The grave also contained a strip bracelet with stamped circle and dot decoration: a repeating motif of a pair of circle and dot stamps followed by a single circle and dot stamp, with notched edges either side of each stamp. The only other site in the whole of my study area with an identical bracelet is Portchester Castle (**49**). The general decorative style, a combination of notches and circle and dot stamps, is found on many British types of bracelet. A bracelet at Oudenburg identical to one at Portchester Castle, with no example exactly the same anywhere else, might be taken as an interesting coincidence, but not conclusive. However, a bracelet from grave 4 at Oudenburg, a strip bracelet with a series of ribbed lines and edge notches to form a repeating pattern, is also unique apart from an identical bracelet at Portchester. The style of this pair, found only at Portchester and Oudenburg, is also British.

Grave 216 at Oudenburg also contained two British bracelets, one with bead imitative decoration, and another with notches along the edges and a line of circle and dot stamps (b3 decoration) (**50**). Finally twisted square sectioned bracelets were found in grave 67 at Oudenburg, and also occur mostly in Britain, including Portchester Castle.

The presence of seven British bracelets with different decorative patterns, two of which can be associated with Portchester Castle or the surrounding area, enables us to suggest that people may have travelled between Portchester and Oudenburg at some point in the late fourth century. The fact that two of the graves at Oudenburg, grave 78 and grave 216, each contained more than one British type, and two of the graves containing foreign material are spatially close to one another in the cemetery, reinforces the argument. We might speculate as to why these people moved across the channel. The most obvious explanation would be that troops from Portchester were sent to Oudenburg, travelling with their family groups. If this is the case, they may have come from Portchester Castle or the surrounding area, or at least obtained much of their jewellery here.

Incidentally, there is also some other unusual material in other graves at Oudenburg, such as tutulus brooches, which are Germanic or Germanic-inspired, as discussed in the previous chapter.

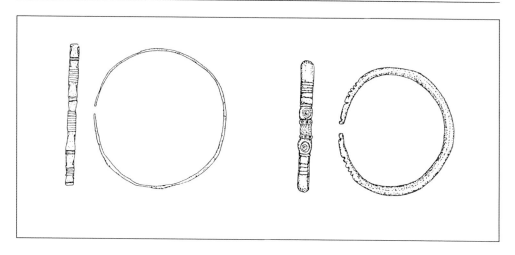

47 British bracelets from Oudenburg, including a bracelet with type 1 snakeshead terminals.
Redrawn after Mertens & Van Impe 1971

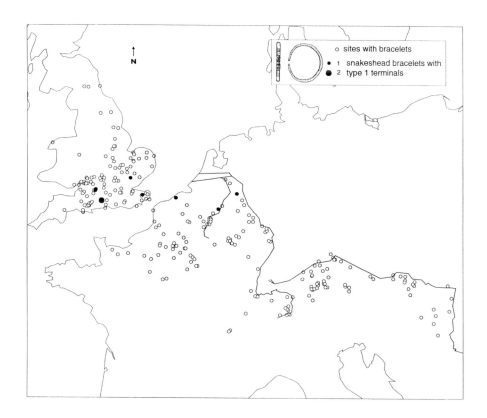

*48 Map of bracelets with type 1 snakeshead terminals found on sites between the Loire and the
Rhine/Danube. This is one of the few snakeshead types to predominate west of the Rhine.*
Copyright Ellen Swift

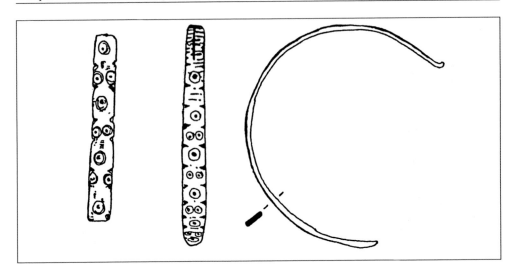

49 Identical bracelets from Oudenburg and Portchester Castle. Redrawn after Mertens & Van Impe 1971 and Cunliffe ed. 1975

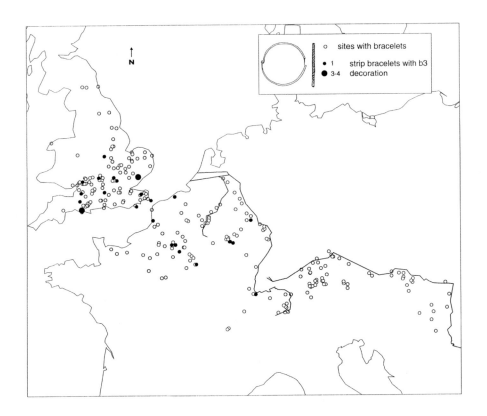

50 Map of bracelets with a line of punched dots separated by pairs of edge notches (see plate 40) found on sites between the Loire and the Rhine/Danube. Copyright Ellen Swift

The Roman frontier

An obvious area of investigation for army movements is the line of the frontier itself. One boundary of the Western Roman Empire followed the Rhine and the Danube through Germany, and is often called the *limes* (limit). The frontier and its development are summarised by King writing on Roman Gaul and Germany. A wooden palisade was established in the first century AD and by the late second century had been developed further, with an added bank and ditch system. Although in the earlier Empire there were attempts to extend the frontier beyond this line, they were never very successful, and the last part of Roman-occupied territory beyond the river line was evacuated in the mid-to-late third century. After this time, the Romans changed their defence policy to a system often called 'defence in depth'. A complex network of military roads, defences and fortifications was constructed behind the frontier line to greet invaders should they breach the frontier itself. Civilians caught in this battle zone could take refuge in hill top settlements, or in flat countryside, in defended towers. The lines of forts, other military posts, settlements, and cemeteries along the Rhine and Danube rivers have been the focus of archaeological research for many years, and they provide a wealth of information.

The Danube frontier

One of the most useful things about objects is that some of them, in particular, crossbow brooches, can be dated to within about 50 years. Crossbow brooches have been studied for many years, particularly by archaeologists working on the Continent, who have placed them in a typological series. By looking at the development of the brooches from one type into the next, they can be placed in a chronological sequence. You could do the same thing today with almost any object type — an example I cited in chapter two was cars. Others might be fashions in clothing, architecture, etc. After putting the brooches in order according to their design, those which occur in coin-dated graves then allow us to suggest more precise date ranges for each brooch type.

Crossbow brooches are widely distributed on sites along the frontiers of the Empire. Taking each type in turn, in chronological order, we can look at how the patterns of distribution vary through time. Assuming that brooches and other objects have not been re-used too often by people other than their original wearers, we can look at where soldiers, officials, and camp-followers were at particular times from the distribution patterns of their brooch, bracelet, buckle types and so on dating to different time spans. The sites where early brooches and other material occur can be plotted, and the resulting distribution compared with the pattern of sites where late brooches and other items are found. This proved to be a useful approach to material found on the Danube frontier in South Germany and Austria. In this area particularly, many brooches occur in secure (undisturbed) contexts of deposition, in graves with the 'military' burial ritual, so that we can be confident that they are buried with the people who wore them in real life. The Danube frontier had a complex system of defence in the fourth century based on large fortresses stationed along the river line, with a network of military roads in the hinterland, defended by smaller forts, watchtowers and fortified hilltop settlements. As well as roads running south from the frontier line, there was also an important road running behind the line of the frontier but parallel to it.

I divided brooches and other objects into groups based on the date ranges which could be suggested from typological analysis. Most of the evidence comes from crossbow brooches which are known to have been worn by the military, and which are present in large numbers on sites in the frontier area. The picture I was able to construct from this evidence is rather complicated, but we can basically watch objects, and by implication people, moving on and off the frontier line at different dates. In simplified version, objects which date to between AD 280 and 320, including early types of crossbow brooches (**51**), show a concentration around the military road running between the important military fortifications of Regensburg and Bregenz. Objects dating to the earlier and middle parts of the fourth century are found both on the river on the frontier line itself and on the roads to the south (**52**), whereas objects which date to the late fourth century and into the fifth century are no longer found on the river line but instead occur predominantly on the line of the military road some way back from, and parallel to, the river (**53**). Towards the end of the fourth century and the beginning of the fifth century, activity declines even on this road. The few objects which have a date range mostly into the fifth century, such as very late crossbow brooches, are not found in the Danube area at all. We seem to be witnessing the gradual withdrawal of people from the frontier area — more specifically, people who were wearing Roman military and even civilian objects.

The evidence suggests that after about AD 350 the frontier line on the river itself may not have been particularly important or well-defended. Towards the end of the fourth century, it might have been abandoned entirely and the main line of defence may have been the road further to the south. One particular type of crossbow brooch, with onion-shaped knobs and slanted engraved lines (\\\\) within a border decorating the bow of the brooch (**54**), is found only on sites along the line of this military road, apart from a single maverick example at Nijmegen in Holland (**55**). If these brooches were all produced within a few years of one another, which seems the most likely explanation for their identical decoration, this correlates with Garbsch's suggestion that a number of fortified settlements in the Danube area were constructed and occupied at the same time by the same groups of soldiers. In turn, the line of the military road behind the frontier appears to have fallen out of use by the fifth century. Written sources of the period say that at more or less the time when military pay to the army ceased, in about AD 410, the Danube provinces virtually collapsed and were subject to very damaging floods and barbarian raids. The archaeological evidence from objects allows us to examine troop movements before any collapse, mapping, possibly, gradual retreat of the Roman defensive line and its ultimate abandonment. Of course this supposes that the people who were wearing crossbow brooches as a mark of military status, who previously occupied these sites, were not merely replaced by non-crossbow brooch wearing military personnel. This could be possible, given the evidence (discussed below) that fifth-century crossbow brooches are not worn by the military. However, all types of object, not just crossbow brooches, drop out of use in the Danube provinces — for example coins, which decline in number rapidly from AD 378 and are almost non-existent by the end of the fourth century. There is some evidence of the continued occupation of some forts in the area in the early fifth century,

51 *Map of objects dating from between AD 280 and 320 in the Danube area.* Copyright Ellen Swift

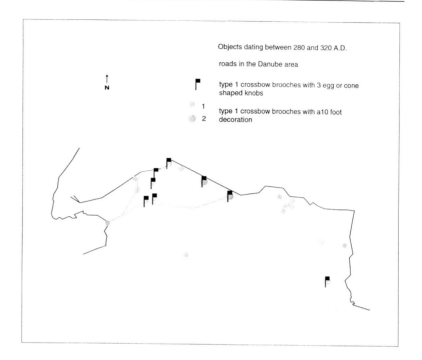

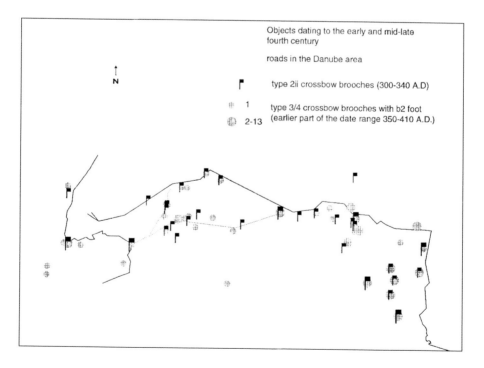

52 *Map of objects dating to the early and mid-fourth century showing concentrations of activity in the frontier zone.* Copyright Ellen Swift

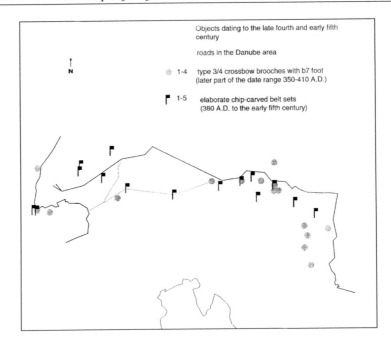

53 Map of objects dating to the end of the fourth century and the beginning of the fifth century showing a shift in areas with concentrated activity. Copyright Ellen Swift

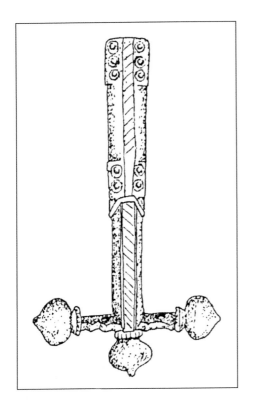

54 Crossbow brooch with e6 bow decoration and b2 foot from Wessling, South Germany. Redrawn after Keller 1971

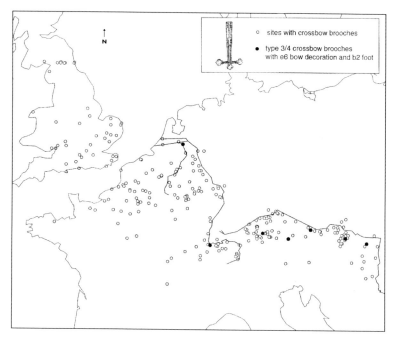

55 *Map of type 3/4 crossbow brooches with e6 bow decoraton (slanted lines left to right between a border of lines) and b2 foot (four circle and dot stamps at the bottom of the foot and six at the top), showing their distribution along the military road running parallel to the frontier in the Danube area.* Copyright Ellen Swift

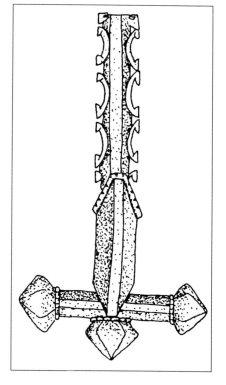

56 *A type 6ii crossbow brooch made from gilded sheet bronze.* Copyright Ellen Swift

for example Windisch in Switzerland and Eining in south Germany, but both of these became fortified settlements with a mostly civilian population rather than remaining as strongly defended military sites. Many other sites fell out of use altogether.

Shifting patterns of distribution — late crossbow brooches

There are noticeable changes in the provincial Roman army material culture of the fourth-fifth century transition period. Crossbow brooches that are being worn in the fifth century are distinctively different from those which are found in the fourth century. As we have seen in the previous chapters, in the mid-to-late fourth century, crossbow brooches were being produced in huge numbers, and were worn by many men in the army. By contrast, fifth-century crossbow brooches are much less common.

Let us examine in more detail one of the latest types of crossbow brooch, type 6 (**56**), which was being manufactured in the fifth century. Many identical brooches of type 6 have been found. These were classified as type 6 in the chronological series by Keller, and, in pages of niggling discussion, which I shall not bore you with here, refined to type 6ii by myself. They were produced between approximately AD 390 and 460. The type is generally quite narrow and delicate in appearance, and is made from sheet metal, which is cut and folded to form a very light, hollow brooch. Earlier crossbow brooches are found in many different materials, including gold, silver, gilt bronze, and copper alloy. Type 6ii occur mostly in gilt bronze, and a few gold examples are known. There is one type of crossbow brooch which has a later date still, type 7 (**colour plate 19**), which, Pröttel suggested, was produced between approximately 460 and 500 AD. This very latest type of crossbow brooch is only found in pure gold and is always decorated with intricate open-work, a difficult technique used by jewellery workshops producing valuable high status ornaments. It has also become much smaller, and therefore more noticeably ornamental than functional.

From these changes we can deduce that fifth-century crossbow brooches were worn only by people of high status, in contrast to the earlier brooches worn at all levels of the hierarchy. This correlates with the trend which is already obvious; that many fewer brooches were being produced in the fifth century. The type of crossbow brooch that is being worn at the beginning of the fifth century has now exclusively become a prestigious, élite item. The contrast between the latest type of crossbow brooch — small, light, hollow, rare, finely decorated, and made from pure gold — and the heavy duty, large, solid, common bronze crossbow brooch being worn in the early-to-mid fourth century is striking. We can use the physical change in the object to suggest changes in the type of person who was likely to have been wearing the brooch.

There is other, art historical evidence that type 6ii and type 7 brooches were worn by men of very high status. For example, the leader of the Roman army in the west in AD 400, Stilicho, is portrayed wearing a type 6ii crossbow brooch on his right shoulder, pinning his cloak, in the diptych of Monza (**57**). A diptych usually consists of two panels hinged together which can be closed like a book. This example is ivory, and is now in the cathedral treasury of Monza. It is interesting that Stilicho's son, shown with his mother on the other panel from the diptych, is also wearing a cloak pinned by a crossbow brooch, though he is clearly no more than a child (**58**). The sixth-century mosaic of the Emperor

57. *Stilicho, as depicted on an ivory panel from the Diptych of Monza, Museo del Duomo, Monza, Italy.* Copyright Ellen Swift

Justinian and his retinue in the church of San Vitale in Ravenna, Italy, is also significant. Although Justininan's retinue has soldiers among it, with shields and spears, they are not wearing crossbow brooches. Instead, crossbow brooches are worn by Justinian's other attendants, who do not look at all soldierly (**cover picture**). In the wall mosaics of St. Apollinaire Nuovo in Ravenna, also of sixth-century date, the scene depicting Christ before Pilate shows Pilate himself, the governor, wearing a crossbow brooch (**colour plate 20**). To the very late Roman, crossbow brooches do not appear to signify simply soldiers, but those of higher status — which ties in with the material evidence of the change from production in base metals to production in gold, or gilt-bronze.

This change in dress customs is also corroborated by the archaeological evidence for the spatial distribution of type 6ii brooches, which mostly date to the fifth century. Until the third quarter of the fourth century crossbow brooches of earlier types appear most often on military sites, particularly along the frontier with free Germany. When we examine the distribution of type 6ii brooches, they no longer have a strong association with the frontier areas, but are scattered more widely inland on settlement and cemetery sites, particularly in France (**59**). This could be because the frontier has now fallen, and is no longer defended by Roman troops. However, in the same period we can see from the presence of other material, including belt sets and weapons, that frontier sites were still occupied on the middle Rhine. Even though new defensive sites, such as the line along the Meuse discussed in the previous chapter, are dated to the fifth century, they are not manned by troops wearing type 6 crossbow brooches, made from AD 390-460. Troops occupying these sites do still wear 'military' belt sets. There is still a military presence in the West, but crossbow brooches are no longer associated with the military. Their shift in distribution away from the frontiers does not show military abandonment of these areas; instead, it is probably linked to a change in use. Crossbow brooches no longer appear to be items of military uniform.

Bringing together all the different strands of evidence, they all suggest that fifth-century crossbow brooches were by this date only worn by very high-status persons in the administration who may have had only a nominal military function, and who were not in 'active service' in the battle zone.

Why did the crossbow brooch become a purely élite item? What does this say about the people wearing these brooches and the transformation of the army after the mid-to-late fourth century? As time progresses, garments and dress accessories often develop the other way, from being worn by the élite to being commonplace items in widespread use. Fashions are introduced by a minority at the top of society, who want us to believe something about their wealth or status or how up-to-the minute they are; everyone else wants to be fashionable too (with the associations that this brings, of wealth and success), so they are copied by others in cheaper versions. As soon as the common people are wearing them, the élite have to distance themselves by introducing something new. However, we have also seen that an item like the toga can move from low status to high status if it becomes associated with the origins of a successful people and therefore a symbol of that people.

Crossbow brooches though, are slightly more complicated. They were always worn by high status persons — early silver brooches with imperial inscriptions are known — and

58. *The wife and child of Stilicho, as depicted on an ivory panel from the Diptych of Monza, Museo del Duomo, Monza, Italy.* Copyright Ellen Swift

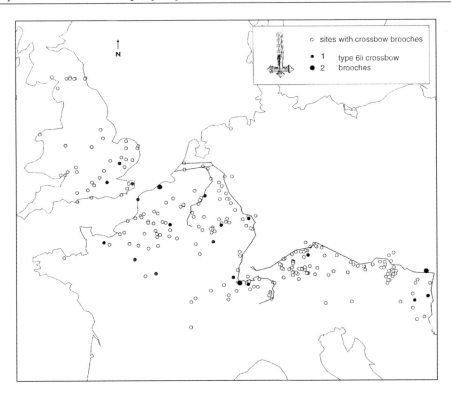

*59. Map showing the distribution of type 6ii crossbow brooches between the Loire and the Rhine/
Danube. Copyright Ellen Swift.*

for many years by those of lower rank as well. Distinctions in the metal used meant that
people still knew, with a glance at the brooch, when they were talking to someone high
up (though it would be difficult to visually distinguish gilt brooches, increasingly found
in the later period, and gold brooches from one another). The existence of high-status
gold, gilt-bronze and silver crossbow brooches might be related to the enhanced status
of the military in the late Roman period. Most Emperors in this period came from a
military background rather than an aristocratic, patrician ancestry. We have already seen
that military dress and court robes replaced the toga for ceremonial occasions in the fifth
century and later. It could be speculated that a military background was now something
to emphasise, something to be proud of — the crossbow brooch and cloak can be worn
by the élite despite, or perhaps because of, their association with the common soldier.

Why did crossbow brooches stop being worn by soldiers? The disuse of crossbow
brooches implies that there were some radical changes in the army and/or the systems in
operation which supplied it. If the military factory for their production was situated in
Pannonia, large-scale production may have ceased when this province was abandoned at
the end of the fourth century. From an earlier chapter, we have seen how the vast majority
of factory-produced brooches were made for soldiers in the Danube provinces. With the
withdrawal of large numbers of troops from the Danube region the factory would go

out of operation. Large-scale production of copper alloy brooches was not transferred to another factory further west. This item of symbolic Roman status was no longer worn by the army. With many troops of Germanic origin, how long could it remain Roman, without a universally recognised uniform?

The Rhine frontier

Since, in the very late period, crossbow brooches are no longer military, we have to turn to other object types to investigate frontier affairs. On the Rhine frontier, we can begin to look at changes in occupation by using the work of Marcus Sommer, who divided up late Roman buckles and belt fittings into different types based on a very fine examination of their decoration. He collected buckles and belt fittings from the whole of the late Western Roman Empire, and compiled a catalogue of the different types found in each area. I used his data to plot maps showing where buckles with a particular type of decoration are found. We have already looked at some of these maps in the previous chapters (**28-9, 42**). Now I want to examine in more detail the distribution of specific types of buckle which are only found in northern Gaul, which date to the late fourth and early fifth century (**60-61**). When I mapped the distribution of some styles of decoration, I found that buckles with particular types of decoration (e.g. Sommer's variation 1c, 2 & 4c) occurred in a linear distribution (**62**). However, this distribution was not along the line of the frontier formed by the Upper Rhine river. Instead, the buckles were found at sites in a line following different rivers: the Meuse and the Sambre. The buckles with these particular styles of decoration did not occur beyond this line, further towards the coast.

Böhme has suggested that the sites along the line of the Meuse-Sambre were a new type of defensive fortified settlement which were built in the early fifth century. The buckles and belt fittings found on this line suggest that, during the years when buckles with this decoration were being worn, military activity may have been concentrated at these sites, rather than sites in the Rhine delta region. Mertens and others have proposed that, because of flooding in the Rhine delta area, by the late fourth century the frontier of the Roman Empire had withdrawn from the line of the lower Rhine, perhaps instead following the line of the fortified Roman road between Bavay and Tongeren. The evidence from Sommer's buckle distributions suggests that the Meuse-Sambre line is another possibility.

One of Sommer's decorative buckle groups (**61**) is distributed *only* on the coastal side of the river, apparently cut off by the line marked out by the buckle types found along the Meuse-Sambre (**colour plate 16**). However, it is not markedly different in style from the types of buckle found on the river line. If you had not wasted away precious years of your life staring at these buckles, you might not be able to tell the difference. Rather than showing the presence of a distinct and different culture in the area beyond the river, this buckle type exhibits the pervasive influence of Roman decorative style and form.

Even more interestingly, I found that some types of late Roman civilian object have a distribution which is noticeably restricted by the line of the Meuse-Sambre. Many object types do not occur beyond it, in the coastal area. These include green hexagonal beads, blue and green biconical beads, blue diamond-faceted beads (**colour plate 21**), some types of beads with trail decoration, and bracelets with multiple motif decoration

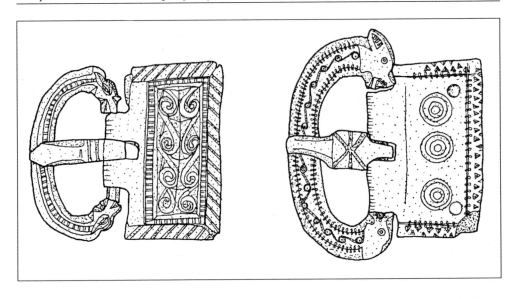

60. Buckles of Sommer's Sorte 1 Form C Typ F Variation 4a. Redrawn after Sommer 1984

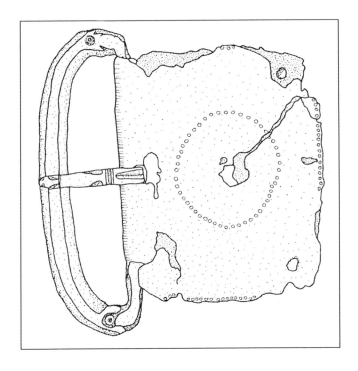

61. Buckles of Sommer's Sorte 1 Form C Typ F Variation 5. Redrawn after Sommer 1984

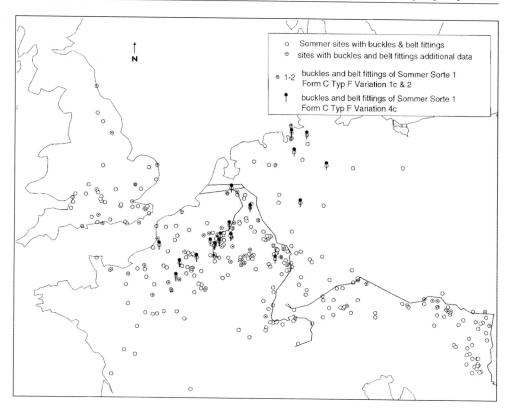

62 Map showing the distribution of Sommer's buckle types Sorte 1 Form C Typ F Variations 1c, 2 & 4c concentrated along the Meuse-Sambre rivers. Copyright Ellen Swift

(**colour plate 22**). One type of bracelet, with a row of circle and dot stamps and single edge notches, avoids an even larger area, apparently cut off by the Bavay-Tongeren road (**colour plate 23**). Unfortunately not many of these types of bracelets and beads are closely datable, but, where good dating evidence is available, they do seem to be found in contexts of a very late date, in the very late fourth century, or, for very recently excavated material, the early fifth century. By this date, then, there is an absence of most types of Roman material culture on the coastal side of the Meuse - Sambre, the line of fortified settlements along the Meuse is clearly marked by the presence of local types of buckles and belt fittings, and the line of the frontier as formed by the lower Rhine may have been less important or even abandoned.

Since many types of Roman beads, bracelets and buckles are no longer found here, the most obvious explanation for the buckles and belt fittings which *are* found in the coastal region might be that they were copies of late Roman buckle types, made by people who no longer had access to the material produced by the workshops which supplied troops on the Meuse-Sambre line, and civilians further south.

There is some historical evidence that the Franks were settled in the area of the Rhine delta, known as Toxandria, by the late fourth century. It is known that important Roman

115

towns in the lower Rhine area such as Köln (Cologne), and, nearby, Maastricht, passed into the hands of Germanic tribes in the late Roman period. By the late fifth century, the Frankish King Childeric had established a kingdom with its centre at Tournai, a town beyond the Meuse-Sambre line. Bringing in evidence from another source, King has studied fifth-century coinage in this area of northern Gaul. Non-Imperial coinage, imitating official Roman coins, clusters around the Meuse-Sambre line. She says that it is impossible to tell whether it is minted by 'barbarians' or by local leaders still trying to represent Rome. The distributions themselves are rather ambiguous, though all types of gold coins (called *solidi*) cluster north of the Meuse-Sambre in the region towards the coast. Both silver with a Trier mint mark (produced by the official Roman mint), and imitations of Trier mint mark silver are found mostly on the south side of the rivers, the area where most other recognisably Roman material is found. It might fit with most of the evidence available to suggest that by the late fourth or early fifth century the area of land actively defended by the Romans had withdrawn to the region demarcated by the river line of the Meuse - Sambre, and that with the resulting breakdown in trade and marketing networks in the area beyond the river, those living here no longer had access to Roman-style material culture as represented by beads, bracelets, and some types of buckles. Consequently late types of beads and bracelets are not found here, and late buckles are only copies of types produced on the other side of the river.

However, the material culture which we see distributed on the south side of the Meuse-Sambre line may not be contemporary with that found beyond this line in the area towards the coast, even if it is only decades earlier. The sole buckle type found in the area beyond the river, towards the coast, is given a very late date range by Sommer, over the whole of the fifth century. Buckles of this type might therefore be later in date than the other objects absent from this area such as bracelets, beads, and other types of buckle. This could account for their differing distribution patterns. They could still be objects worn by ostensibly Roman troops (though these definitions are starting to seem a little irrelevant). Of course, this does not solve the problem of why many types of objects, and not merely a few buckle types, are absent from the coastal area.

It seems to me that many of the problems of interpreting archaeological evidence come from a fundamental inability to refine dating sufficiently, so that the evidence from the ground is not merely a tangle of remnants from successive events. How can you compare the spatial distribution of two object types if you do not know for sure that they were produced at the same time? Even if you can date both to the second half of the fifth century, how do you know that one was not produced between 350 and 370 and the other was not only in vogue from 390-400? Using the stylistic development of objects we can sometimes refine dating sufficiently to separate out patterning into quite small time periods, as we have seen for the object distributions in the Danube area. This area was much easier, because we were dealing mainly with the fourth century; the evidence is better, and the dating is better. Ideally, we would wait until chronology was very refined before trying to do anything with the spatial patterning of contemporary object types. But of course, this is archaeology, the evidence is never going to be flawless, so we have to do the best we can with what is available at the moment, and hope that future research will add to or alter the picture we have been painfully trying to build up.

The patterns in the material in this area of northern France and Belgium in the late fourth and fifth century are fascinating, representing as they do the activity of the final Roman troops based there, and the interactions between the military and civilian occupants of the area. As we have seen from the distribution of material on the Danube, South Germany, Austria and Hungary east of the Danube area had been abandoned by the early fifth century. Activity on the Danube can be seen in the way material retreats from the frontier line and finally ceases to be found altogether. By the early fifth century, the focus of attention shifts towards the West, to France and Belgium. If anywhere is crucial in the end of the Roman Western Empire, this area is. Here, too, we can see a great deal of frantic activity in the frontier area, new fortifications, possibly a retreat to a new frontier line, and the erosion of Roman-style material culture. Remaining members of an ostensible 'Roman' army are no longer wearing an identical, accepted uniform of crossbow brooch and belt set, but locally-produced buckles and belt fittings found only in small regional areas. Crossbow brooches are now worn only by the élite, and their distribution has shifted away from the frontiers to the far west of France. By the early fifth century, some areas have apparently fallen outside the marketing zone of workshops producing late Roman beads, buckles and belt fittings.

We can read about the end of the West in historical accounts, and now we can see the patterns in the material changing in response to the events of the final years of Roman rule in the West. Paradoxically, the archaeological evidence only makes clear how complex those events actually were.

5   The End of the West and beyond

Once the Roman authorities had lost political control of the West, with the frontiers abandoned, the army changed out of all recognition, and, with Germanic rulers in charge, it might be assumed that Roman influence was at an end, replaced by Germanic practices and culture. However, the split between the Roman and post-Roman period is not that well defined in the material record. It has already become clear that sometimes it is hard to distinguish between Germanic peoples and Romans, and that there was a considerable cultural exchange between the two groups in the late fourth century. Similarly, it is often forgotten that many aspects of medieval culture (particularly religious culture) were heavily dependent on late antique precedents. In the fifth century, did Roman culture continue among the local population who were now ruled by Germanic overlords? Did Roman dress styles and practices live on among any sectors of the population? Is the End through material really an end?

'Provincial Roman' dress begins to change in the fourth century. There are complaints in contemporary sources that people are adopting barbaric customs such as the wearing of trousers. New items begin to creep into the normal repertoire of objects recovered from a cemetery. Still in the fourth century, within the Roman Empire, composite triangular single-sided bone combs (**63**) begin to occur with greater frequency, alongside the more common double-sided simple and composite types (**64**). As discussed in chapter two, blue square beads with diamond-shaped facets become one of the most popular types of bead found on necklaces and bracelets in late Roman cemeteries. Opaque annular beads with swirly and squiggly patterns are found in increasing numbers towards the end of the fourth century (as discussed in chapter three), and before this have not occurred within the Empire since the pre-Roman period.

All of these objects new to the dress fashions of the provincial Roman population are items which were once found exclusively beyond the frontiers in the Germanic homelands. Once they start appearing within the Empire, it is rather difficult to find out where they were made, but there is certainly evidence that by the end of the fourth century some of them were being produced within the Empire. A workshop for the production of opaque beads with trail decoration in different colours, already mentioned in chapter three, was for example excavated at Trier, and dates to the end of the fourth century.

Shoes with hobnails (introduced by the Romans, and present throughout the Empire) are by the end of the fourth century supplanted by sewn leather shoes. Carol Van Driel Murray has carried out extensive research on shoes, and concludes that new types of sewn shoe are introduced even earlier, in the third century (**65**). They are also worn in the fourth century and later. Shoes of this kind can be seen on the mosaics depicting the

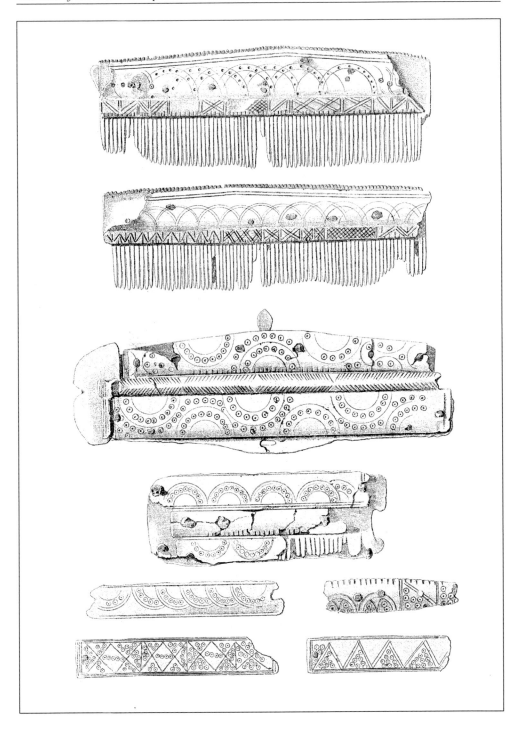

63 *Single-sided triangular bone combs, from a German antiquarian volume, 'Der Altertümer*
unserer Heidnischen Vorzeit' (Antiquities of our Pagan Prehistory) by L. Lindenschmidt,
Volume 1 (1858) Heft XII Taf 6. Copyright Society of Antiquaries of London

64. *A double-sided bone comb with punched circle and dot decoration found in a grave at the Lankhills cemetery, Winchester.* Redrawn after Griffiths in Clarke 1979

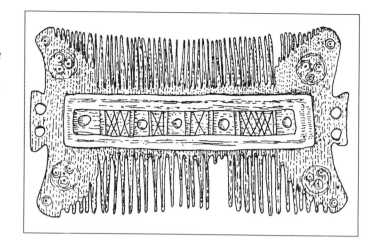

65 *Sewn leather shoes from Welzheim of a new type which were introduced in the third century.* Redrawn after Planck 1977

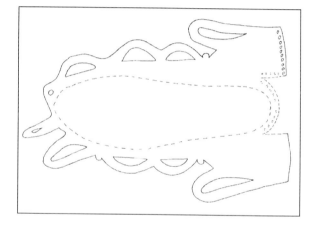

Emperor Justinian in Ravenna and are worn by Stilicho on the diptych of Monza. They are cut to a pattern in a completely innovative way; the sole and the upper are cut out in one piece and the upper is then folded and sewn into place, forming a shoe which covers most of the foot. The method is apparently the same as that used to construct leather shoes in the early medieval period.

The new bead types and other dress accessories mentioned above appear to have become part of general provincial late Roman fashions by the end of the fourth century, worn by the same members of the population who continued to wear other characteristically 'Roman' items. This marks them out from other 'Germanic' material (such as tutulus brooches) which is found only in small quantities within the Empire and which often has grave associations with other unusual material or uncommon burial practices. However, some archaeologists such as Halsall would suggest that tutulus brooches, once indisputably Germanic, may also have become part of local rather than specifically Germanic dress fashions.

The objects commonly found in fourth-century cemeteries which previously occurred only in free Germany, and those which were new innovations in the third century, continued to be produced and worn in the fifth century. Their appearance within the Empire in significant numbers, and the way they flourished alongside established Roman fashions even in the fourth century, indicate the extent to which new dress styles were to replace many elements of Roman-style dress in the fifth century. We can begin to investigate the survival of Roman items of dress, and new innovations in the fifth century, by examining the fifth century grave of the Frankish king Childeric.

Childeric's grave at Tournai

Childeric ruled over the Germanic successor kingdom in northern France. Under his authority, some aspects of Roman culture still continued to thrive. It is known that Childeric considered himself to be the direct inheritor of Roman governance, legitimated by the Eastern Roman Emperor who still ruled in Constantinople (Istanbul). I have already mentioned the latest type of crossbow brooch, type 7, produced in pure gold in the second half of the fifth century. Not many type 7 brooches exist, especially not from areas which were by now Germanic hegemonies, though there is a significant hoard from North Africa called the Ténès hoard; most occur in Italy. There are only two from the area of the former Western Empire covered by this study: the brooch found in Childeric's grave at Tournai in Belgium [now known only from drawings and replicas (**colour plate 24**), since the original brooch is lost], and an identical brooch from Innsbruck. The curator at Tournai museum told me that the Innsbruck brooch is probably a copy of the Childeric brooch (or the brooch itself, since it has disappeared from Tournai) made during the Second World War, when France and Belgium were occupied, and taken to Austria. Childeric's grave goods have been a potent symbol of French nationalism for centuries. As mentioned in the introductory chapter, Napoleon had his ceremonial robes embroidered with motifs from Childeric's grave goods. The Innsbruck copy might be regarded as a German attempt to appropriate Childeric, who was after all a Germanic king. We can see how objects continue to have a significance for future centuries well beyond the meaning with which they were originally endowed.

Returning to Antiquity, we can consider the possible significance of the brooch's presence in Childeric's grave. Its grave position is unfortunately not known, since the grave was excavated in the seventeenth century. At this time, the brooch was not recognised, and was suggested to be a pen, or stylus. There is even a helpful drawing in an early publication of someone holding it to write with, with the pin of the brooch extended to form a nib. The presence of the brooch in the king's grave, and a total absence of crossbow brooches in any other graves of the period in northern Gaul, perhaps implies that he was aware of its symbolic meaning. It might be suggested that Childeric is expressing his supposed Roman authority through wearing or being buried with a high-status Roman crossbow brooch.

Apart from the brooch in Childeric's grave, apparently so full of symbolic significance, and which was presumably worn with reference to Roman dress customs, in the fifth century brooches were not generally worn by Germanic men. In Germanic culture, as already mentioned, brooches were a common item of female dress. They were used to pin the tunic on each shoulder, and were therefore worn, and occur in graves, in pairs. The crossbow brooch fell out of use by the end of the fifth century in the areas of the Western Empire which were occupied by Germanic tribes. Cross-shaped bow brooches with knobs at the terminals are found in non-Roman contexts, for example in Anglo-Saxon female graves. There have been some unconvincing attempts to link these and other types of post-Roman brooches with the crossbow brooch itself, with the suggestion that they developed from Roman brooches after the end of the Roman Empire in the West. However, there are so many confusing cross-pollinations of influence that it is difficult to disentangle one from another.

It seems to be the case from other object types that Roman influence on Germanic culture outside the Empire, in the fourth century, was more significant. In this period, small numbers of Roman objects reached trading sites beyond the frontiers. Aspects of style borrowed from the Romans were then developed in comparative isolation before they were re-introduced into the West in the migration period. By this time, their style had drifted so far away from any Roman prototypes as to be almost unrecognisable. The most commonly cited example is Nydam-style ornament, found on brooches in Scandinavia. In the earliest examples, designs decorating brooches are based on Roman motifs. Animals and human faces are often combined with geometric ornament in panels (**66**), similar to the style of fourth century Roman metalwork (**16, 45**). Fish-tailed creatures are frequently used; composite land-sea animals are a common feature of late Roman art. The fish-tailed creatures might also be based on popular Roman motifs such as dolphins. The designs are probably taken from contemporary fourth-century buckles and belt fittings that found their way to Scandinavia in small quantities. However the motifs quickly develop into something very different. This may be because those copying each motif did not know what it represented. It is much easier to copy something accurately if you know what it is, because the lines make sense and form a picture. If, however, they appear to be an abstract collection of marks, a copyist will view them differently (think about optical illusions) and will reproduce them just as lines, rather than depicting a coherent image. On the other hand, perhaps the deliberate intent of the craftsperson was to create something new, merely using the Roman prototype as an idea from which to create a style that was intentionally very different. By the time Nydam-style brooches travel back within the Roman Empire, brought by the Angles and Saxons migrating to England in the fifth century and later, the motifs have developed into something new, and look totally different from provincial Roman decoration.

It seems far more likely then, that Anglo-Saxon brooches with knobs at their terminals developed from female brooches being worn in the Germanic homelands, which may have had some earlier input from Roman styles, rather than developing directly from fifth-century crossbow brooches worn by the male military Roman population within the Empire. The crossbow brooch worn by men and Germanic brooch styles worn by women therefore remain separate. Germanic men do not copy Childeric and start to wear the Roman crossbow brooch. The crossbow brooch did not have any obvious influence on Germanic brooch styles. Crossbow brooches therefore ultimately came to a dead end, though they did survive for a time in areas still under Roman rule. As symbols of Roman authority it is appropriate that they did not long outlive the end of the Roman Empire in the West.

Gold barbarian bracelets

Changes in style and in the way objects were worn in the post-Roman period are also apparent when we examine what happened to bracelets in the fifth century. Again, the investigation begins by using Childeric's tomb (d. AD 482). In addition to the crossbow brooch and other material, a gold bracelet was found in the tomb, beautifully illustrated by Chiflet in 1655 (**colour plate 19**) though again its exact burial position is not known. The bracelet was simple in form, a penannular ring with no visible decoration on the surfaces. However it did have characteristic thickened ends, as though someone had rolled out a cylinder from the metal, which got thinner in the middle (remember those early experiences with Plasticine?). The cylinder was then bent round in a circle which could be slipped on a wrist. Bracelets of this type are usually called '*Kolbenarmringe*' after the German name (*Kolben* means 'butt' and refers to the terminals). Kolbenarmringe are unlike any contemporary Roman/Byzantine bracelet. Very late Roman and Byzantine gold bracelets are usually flat, with cut open-work. Fourth-century Roman copper alloy bracelets are more similar, and undecorated bracelets with penannular terminals were certainly worn at this time, but they did not have thickened ends. In any case, all of these styles of Roman bracelet would be worn by women, not men.

Gold bracelets with thickened ends appear in other post-Roman graves (**67**), roughly contemporary with Childeric's grave, in both the area formerly within the Roman Empire and in some regions beyond. They are not very common. Unfortunately many of the bracelets from the post-Roman period which do exist have lost their original grave contexts, as they were excavated in the nineteenth century and earlier. When we try to examine the way in which these bracelets were worn at burial, unfortunately no precise details exist from Childeric's tomb. If we investigate the slight evidence we have of other graves which are definitely from the fifth century, and which were well-excavated and recorded, we do find some people — usually women — still buried with different types of bracelets, and some even wearing bracelets one on either wrist. This, of course, is how they would have been worn in life, though not in death, by a provincial Roman population. For example, there is a fifth-century female grave at Éprave in Belgium containing two flat penannular bracelets with circle and dot motifs. These would not look too out of place in a late Roman cemetery, though they are made from silver rather than copper alloy. At Domolospuszta, there is a woman wearing two bracelets of the type found in Childeric's tomb — gold with thickened ends. One bracelet is found on either wrist, worn according to the usual provincial Roman dress custom. If we look at all the contexts in which *Kolbenarmringe* have been found, it is noticeable that they occur in the fifth century in gold, silver, and copper alloy, and that they are often found in female graves. Where the grave context is known, they sometimes have an association with the left wrist. One *Kolbenarmring* which may have been worn by a man is the gold bracelet from the tomb discovered in Pouan in 1842. Though precise grave details have been lost, the other items in the grave group are all objects which are found in male burials — gold buckles, a gold ring, a sword, and a scramasax (a kind of double edged axe used as a weapon). The

66 *Silver and niello motif in Nydam style (Schleswig, Germany) with decoration derived from Roman motifs.* Redrawn after Salin 1935

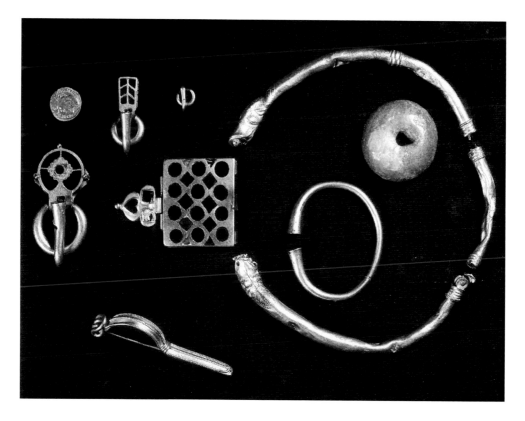

67 *Group of jewellery from Wolfsheim, Germany, including a gold 'Kolbenarmringe' centre.* Copyright Museum Wiesbaden

specifically male association suggested for *Kolbenarmringe* by their presence in Childeric's grave is probably parallelled in this burial, therefore, but not borne out more widely by other fifth-century examples.

Is the bracelet in the tomb of the Frankish king merely an anomaly? In the very early Roman period in Italy, the male gold bracelet was known — it was worn to signify warrior status in the first century and before. Early Roman ceremonial-style bracelets are different from the bracelets with thickened ends found in free Germany. Because they were not worn after about the first century, it seems very unlikely that Childeric's bracelet has anything to do with Roman customs. The other obvious place to look is free Germany (the area outside Roman jurisdiction in the Roman period). Though there is no evidence from the fourth century, Werner has shown that in the third century bracelets were worn by Germanic men on the right wrist. Not only that, but they are identical bracelets to the one in Childeric's grave — i.e. *Kolbenarmringe* made of gold. Werner plotted their distribution in free Germany in the third century and their movement further west in the fifth century (**68**) He suggested that the bracelets had a symbolic value. The right wrist is significant because this was the sword arm. Werner proposed that the bracelets indicated warrior status among the Germanic tribes. Perhaps both the early Roman custom and the Germanic practice ultimately derived from a pre-Roman 'Celtic' tradition which was common throughout Europe.

Though there are very few datable examples of gold bracelets, it seems to be the case that those datable to 400-450 are found in the east, modern-day eastern Europe, while those dating to 450-500 occur in the west, in the Rhineland, Belgium and northern France. They appear to be moving the same way as most of the migrating peoples of this period. The presence of gold bracelets chronologically earlier in eastern Europe is perhaps related to their source, or the source of the gold from which they were made.

Werner analysed the weight of Roman gold coins, solidi (**colour plate 25**) and of gold *Kolbenarmringe*. He found that the bracelets' weight could be divided up into whole numbers corresponding to the weight of a number of solidi, coins issued in pure gold. For example, Childeric's bracelet from Tournai equals the weight of 67 gold solidi, whereas the bracelet from Pouan in Germany appears to have been made from 38 gold solidi. Appropriately enough, the bracelet from the king's tomb is almost twice as valuable. Gold was used mostly to pay the army, and it is also known from written sources that the Romans sometimes tried to keep the barbarians in the east at bay by paying them off. Barbarian raiders would usually be given gold coins, solidii, as the other Roman coins in use would be worthless to them, having only a nominal value (as the paper in bank notes has no intrinsic value). There are also some references in the sources to gold bracelets rather than solidi being doled out to keep barbarians quiet. (You would have thought that it would not take a master of diplomacy to see that this policy was likely to be self defeating, actually encouraging the barbarians to mill about in a threatening way on the frontiers.)

The presence of gold *Kolbenarmringe*, and possibly other types of gold bracelets as well, could therefore perhaps be linked to the availability of gold coin in various areas at this time. Another example of the practice of making bracelets from coins might be the silver bracelets which were produced in Poland in the second century and later, and which were possibly made from denarii.

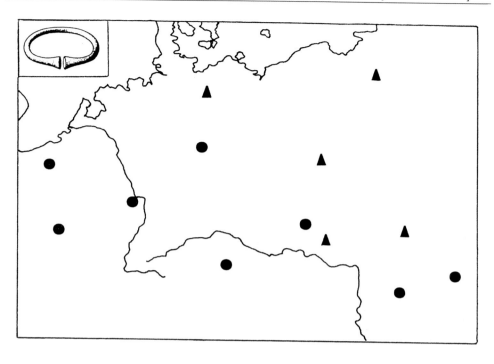

68 Distribution of gold Kolbenarmringe in the third century (represented by triangles) and the fifth century (represented by circles). Redrawn after Werner 1980

As mentioned already, gold *Kolbenarmringe* disappear from view in the fourth century in free Germany, and we do not know if they were still worn or if they continued to be worn in the same way. Their reappearance in the fifth century, within the former Empire, suggests that they did not fall out of use, and that there is merely a problem with the archaeological evidence from the fourth century, though of course we have no way of knowing if they continued to be worn only by male warriors on the right wrist. Has their symbolism remained the same throughout this period, from the third century to the fifth century? The example from Childeric's tomb would suggest that gold *Kolbenarmringe* were still associated with male warrior status. Though Childeric is the only known fifth-century example of *Kolbenarmringe* in a male grave, and the custom seems to be dying out, it might be expected that Childeric would be one of its last exponents if we consider the way in which, today, archaic customs of dress have lingered on among royalty and the nobility for ceremonial occasions, when they have long since fallen out of use in everyday dress.

Checking the evidence from the historical sources which were written in this period, we find within them references to gold objects being made by craftsmen working for the Germanic ruling class (Eugippius' *Life of Saint Severinus*, written in about 511 AD). Gold bracelets are specifically referred to as being in the gift of the ruler by one source. Gregory of Tours, writing rather later, in the sixth century, refers in his volume on the history of the Franks to a bribe of gold arm-bands and sword-belts given by Childeric's son, Clovis, when he was king (Book II, p.157, tr. & ed. Thorpe 1974). The association of gold bracelets with sword belts in this paragraph might suggest a continued link with warrior status.

In addition to the symbol of Roman authority, the gold crossbow brooch, it is interesting that Childeric is carrying a symbol of warrior status known from the Germanic homelands, the gold *Kolbenarmringe*. He also has an heirloom bag of Roman *denarii* which were present in free Germany in the second century. The ruler of the supposedly turbulent transition period between Roman and Frankish dominion redoubles the force of his authority by appropriating as many symbols of power as possible. Former Roman citizens would recognise the crossbow brooch and be familiar with its meaning. Germanic people present within the Empire might not recognise the brooch and what it represented, but would be able to easily interpret and acknowledge the message inherent in a Germanic gold bracelet. I talked in chapter one of this book about the use of jewellery as the symbol of belonging to a group. Here we see clearly the use of jewellery in a symbolic way in late Antiquity, to reinforce the power and legitimacy of the king to every group of people under his authority.

Bracelets in the sixth century and later

With migration, customs from the mother country tend to become altered or corrupted when they continue in a new land to which people have emigrated (for example, the head flattening practice which we looked at in an earlier chapter which eventually died out at Fontenay). The practice of men wearing gold bracelets on the wrist of the sword arm is no exception. By the fifth century we have seen that this practice is apparently falling out of use. Through time, the bracelet completely lost its male warrior associations. It can hardly continue to be the symbol of macho status when women have started wearing it, and might give the wrong impression entirely. By the sixth century it had become a female item of dress worn mostly on the left wrist, as a study by Koch has shown, and different styles of *Kolbenarmringe* continued to develop (**69**).

Bracelets for women in the sixth century were not as popular as they had been in the Roman period. Koch, for example, considered that bracelets from this period were still a symbol of high status, as gold Kolbenarmringe had evidently been in the fifth century and earlier. They were still made from precious metal, though now mainly produced in silver rather than gold. It is interesting that with the change in gender association the metal which the bracelet is made from also changed, and that it also swapped from being placed on the right wrist to a position on the left wrist. This kind of male/female opposition is commonly documented in anthropological studies; repeating patterns of symbolism frequently consist of pairs of opposites, men taking one pole, and women the other. For example, men might be linked to the sun (a male god, perhaps) and women to the moon (a goddess). From here it is not too much of a jump to associate gold, sun colour, with men, and silver, moon colour, with women. These associations also perpetuate the idea of women as less important or negative, and the dominance of men (gold more valuable

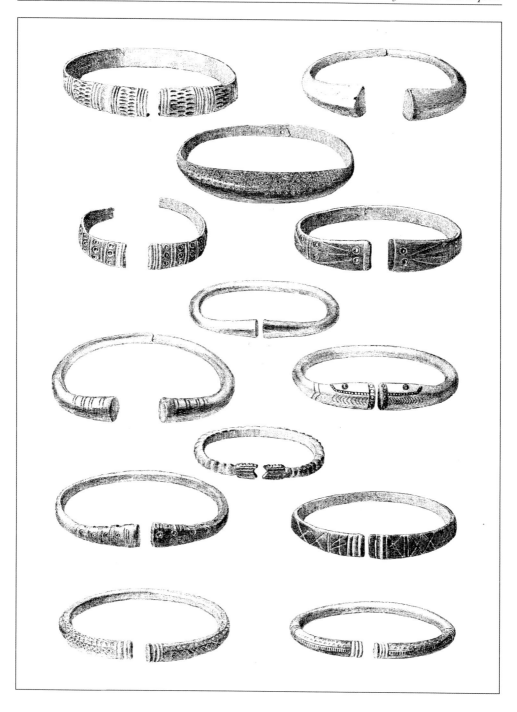

69 *Several different types of fifth- and sixth-century Kolbenarmringe found in Germany, from a German antiquarian volume, 'Der Altertumer unserer Heidnischen Vorzeit' (Antiquities of our Pagan Prehistory) by L. Lindenschmidt, Volume 1 (1858) Heft XII Taf 6.* Copyright Society of Antiquaries of London

than silver, day and sunlight are positive, knowable things, whereas the night brings darkness, mystery, and uncertainty). Similarly, if the right wrist became male associated, as the sword was carried in the right hand, the opposite hand would immediately become female. More prosaically, of course, the change to production in silver could have been due to a shortage of gold. Gold apparently became rarer by the seventh century, when coins previously made from gold begin to be produced in silver. What caused the initial transition from male to female object is of course not known. (Perhaps the men refused to wear silver bracelets, bringing the two explanations together). It may be linked to disruptions in culture caused by the migration from the Germanic homelands, and not least the residual influence of Roman culture, in which bracelets were a female item.

Britain of course is different. It was not settled by Franks but by people, from Denmark as well as northern Germany, and the bracelets with thickened ends do not take off here at all. Instead, bracelets remain extremely rare in Anglo-Saxon contexts for the whole of the period. There are, however, some similarities to the continental Germanic sixth-century custom. Where bracelets are found, they are usually silver, and seem to be worn by women on the left wrist most frequently. They are usually simple wire bracelets with an expanding fastening, a type popular in the Roman period, though in the Anglo-Saxon period these wire loops were also used for girdle hangers, so unless they are worn at burial it is a bit difficult to be sure whether they are bracelets or not. Even residual copper alloy Roman bracelets, which sometimes occur in Anglo-Saxon graves, are likely to be worn on the left wrist.

From the production of *Kolbenarmringe* and other types of bracelet in silver in the sixth century there is an inevitable decline into widespread production in bronze, at which point these bracelets presumably lost any high-status associations they once had. *Kolbenarmringe* continued to be worn for many centuries, with increasing variations of the style developing. They eventually change from solid cast bracelets to flat strip bracelets that widen in only one dimension at the terminal. Decoration becomes more frequent and complex. In the seventh-century cemetery at Gondorf in Germany, 50 percent of the female burials still contain one bracelet, implying that it was still a common practice to wear them on the left wrist only. However, by the tenth century, any association with the left wrist appears to have been lost, and bracelets are often worn in pairs. This pattern appears to be a common life-cycle for decorative objects, as discussed in the previous chapter. They are introduced by an élite, and are predominantly status symbols, produced in expensive materials and therefore restricted to the people who can afford to pay for those materials. As the objects become familiar and desirable they are copied in less expensive materials and worn by a greater number of the general population, eventually becoming both common and cheap, but not necessarily retaining much similarity to the original item. Any symbolism they may once have had is eroded or disappears completely and new meanings emerge. By the tenth century bracelets seem to be worn again as they were under the Romans, as decorative jewellery for the female population at large, without any status associations.

To summarise, late Roman bracelets seem not to have survived very well in the fifth century and their production had definitely stopped quite early on in this century. Some Germanic bracelets and residual Roman material were worn in continuing Roman style, some Germanic and Roman bracelets in Germanic style. There is no clear division in the material between fourth-century Roman-style heirlooms being worn in a Roman fashion and new Germanic precious metal bracelets being worn in Germanic fashion. Instead, from the limited evidence available, there seems to be considerable overlap. The most significant trend is that bracelets settle down to being purely female items of dress again by about the sixth century, though there may be problems ascertaining the original context of use of gold bracelets.

Perhaps, at the turn of the fifth century, there was initially a continuing demand for copper alloy bracelets which could not be supplied due to general disruption, or perhaps changes in fashion, partly resulting from the Germanic influx, dictated that bracelets were no longer in demand apart from among the élite. There seems to have been an unsuccessful attempt to continue production of Roman-style bracelets in the very early fifth century. For most of the fourth century, it appears to be the case that separate workshops were responsible for the production of different items such as bracelets and buckles. However, very late styles of bracelets and belt set which date to the early fifth century sometimes share the same decorative motifs and details of technique. This could have resulted from the closing down of established bracelet workshops. Buckle workshops appear to have taken over the production of bracelets, though these bracelets are rare and the trend seems not to have been long-lived.

It is too easy, however, to dismiss the cessation of Roman-style culture among the civilian population as an inevitable result of significant disruptions to the systems of trade and marketing which occurred at the fall of the Western Empire, connected with pay ceasing to the army and coin production stopping in the West. It seems likely that there were such disruptions. In Britain, the cessation of coinage was accompanied by the disuse, or a change in use, of trade and redistribution centres such as the towns. The pottery industries in Britain had all been extremely successful in the fourth century and towards its end production was booming. In the fifth century the pottery industries apparently collapsed. They may have been dependent on established trade networks. However, we do not know to what extent goods were also exchanged in a bartering system which would not be dependent on coinage. In the same period, large numbers of horsehead buckles were apparently being produced and distributed with little difficulty. Their distribution is mainly in the south-west, as is the distribution of late beads. It appears that in this area it was very much business as usual.

On the Continent, disruptions in trade and marketing systems could account for the absence of late Roman material in the area between the Meuse-Sambre and the coast. Roman material culture, however, including buckles produced by thriving workshops, continued in production to the south of this line, into at least the mid-fifth century, and perhaps even to the end of the fifth. Buckles and belt fittings have later date ranges than any other type of Roman personal ornament. There is some evidence that the types of production centres for these objects were changing both on the Continent and in Britain in the very late fourth century. Böhme has shown that buckle and belt set manufacture changed from a few large workshops in the fourth century to many small production centres by the fifth century. These production centres seem to have flourished for much of the fifth century in the Rhineland and northern Gaul. New styles of animal ornament and new types of buckles and belt fittings, which owe something to the Roman tradition, continue in production in the sixth century and beyond. Animal ornament remains a popular motif (**70**). Early medieval strap ends (the tag at the end of a belt) are also often based on a common Roman shape for strap-ends, which resembles an amphora (**71**).

It seems that where there was still a demand for Roman-style objects, they continued to be produced, though now in small regional workshops rather than larger production centres trading across wide areas. It is interesting that the Roman tradition survives in male dress accessories and other items such as vessels rather than female dress accessories. Surviving female dress accessories from the fourth century are of course all the items of dress which were ultimately Germanic in derivation, and which only became popular in the late Roman period, such as wavy trail beads and composite triangular single-sided bone combs. Sewn one-piece leather shoes, the sole folded up around the edges to form the upper, which were new to Roman fashion in the third century, survived beyond the fourth century. The latter two objects could easily be produced in very small workshops or even by individual craftsmen and would therefore not be dependent on a distribution system. Changes in dress style seem to be partly resulting from changes in supply mechanisms, though these must also be directly dependent on fluctuations in demand.

New types of dress accessory

There are some indications of wholly new insular styles in jewellery — some kinds of pins and necklaces, for example — developing in the very late Roman period and during the fifth century. Some of these, from the very sparse evidence so far accumulating, seem to have been restricted to very small areas. For example, in the excavation of the late Roman cemetery at Ickham in Kent in the last few years, a large number of pendants — nine in total — were found which did not seem to have an exact parallel anywhere else in Roman Britain, until another pendant of this type was recently discovered at the nearby site of Wickenborough, also in Kent. These pendants are characterised by decoration of figures and animals on both the back and the front, and some are set with an imitation glass jewel. Henig, who discusses the pendant's placement in late and post-Roman jewellery styles, says that the glass settings have some parallels with pendants dating to the fifth century and later found as far away as Rome and St. Petersburg. Some aspects of their decoration, however, are similar to that on post-Roman objects in Kent and Sussex, which are decorated in a manner known as the 'Quoit brooch style'.

There is no general consensus on the origins of the Quoit brooch style. It is named after the type of jewellery on which it most often appears, ring-shaped brooches found mostly in early Anglo-Saxon contexts. They are decorated with a distinctive animal ornament style of four-legged animals and geometric decoration. The style is found mostly in Britain, though it also occurs on a few finds in France. A particularly characteristic feature is the representation of furry animals, the fur characterised using hatches or patterns of nicks. The origin of the style has been variously argued to be Scandinavian, Anglo-Saxon, Frankish, and post-Romano-British, though recent opinion tends towards the post-Romano-British explanation. The geometric patterns and animal ornament can be suggested to have developed from the decorative style of late Roman

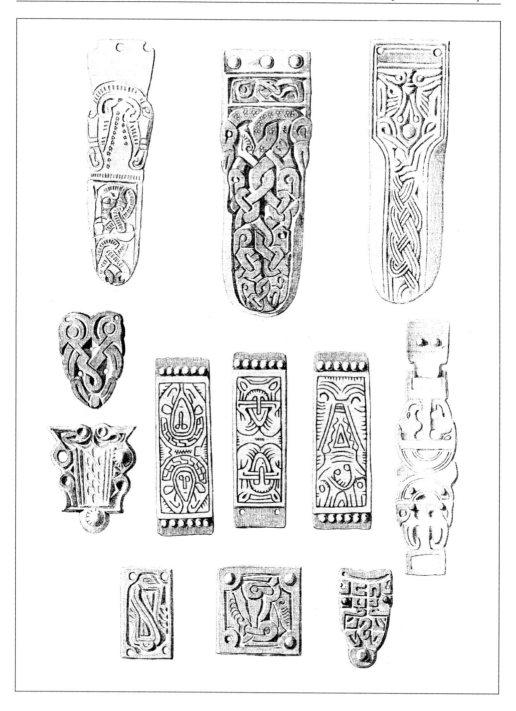

70 *Animal ornament on early medieval strap-ends, from a German antiquarian volume, 'Der Altertümer unserer Heidnischen Vorzeit' (Antiquities of our Pagan Prehistory) by L. Lindenschmidt, Volume 1 (1858) Heft III Taf 8.* Copyright Society of Antiquaries of London

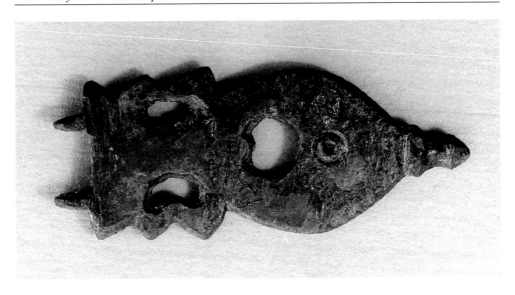

71 Amphora-shaped strap end found at the very large late Roman cemetery at Ickham, Kent, which has been recently excavated. Copyright Canterbury Archaeological Trust

buckles and belt-fittings. In Britain, such late Roman material was itself developing a distinctive insular style in the very late fourth/early fifth century (see chapter two). In this insular style of double-sided horsehead buckles with long plates, hatched motifs are invariably found on the plate. However, horsehead buckles have a differing distribution to quoit brooch style, in the south-west of Britain. Quoit brooch style could also be argued to have a more convincing derivation from stylistic aspects of Continental late Roman metalwork. This would not necessarily preclude a British origin for the style, since Continental material found in Britain is concentrated in the south-east, with a roughly parallel distribution to objects of the quoit brooch style. If you are now thoroughly confused, you can appreciate the difficulties faced by archaeologists working on the fifth century, who often have to argue from difficult evidence like this which has to be considered very carefully.

Developments such as quoit brooches, the quoit brooch style, and the unusual pendants from Ickham are difficult to analyse and seem to have originated under the influence of more than one stylistic tradition. They do, however, show that jewellery styles and fashions of dress in southern Britain were continuing to develop, perhaps towards an insular British style, in a distinctive way from the end of the Roman period into the early fifth century. This is in spite of the fact that the new types of object and styles of decoration quickly became subsumed under more dominant kinds of brooches and other jewellery, decorated with more stylised animal ornament, which are best paralleled in the Scandinavian homelands from which the Anglo-Saxons originally came.

Apart from buckles and belt fittings, then, by the mid-fifth century, 'provincial Roman' dress accessories, and therefore styles of dress which were based on normal provincial Roman costume, seem eventually to be replaced wholesale by 'Germanic' fashions — the dress customs of the Germanic homelands. An interim period also seems to exist in some areas with unusual new items developing under a range of influences. By the mid-to-late fifth century, however, there are large numbers of burials in Germanic-style dress with distinctive brooches and other jewellery. In the past, this has been interpreted as a large scale Germanic influx into the various countries. The remaining Romano-British seem to have become archaeologically less visible, although, as discussed in the introductory chapter, settlements with residual Roman objects which might have been used by the native population have often been dated to the fourth century when they might actually be rather later.

It could also be the case, however, that the resident population actually adopted 'Germanic' dress style themselves. As we have seen, some Germanic-style objects had already become popular items of dress among the general population in the fourth century, before the main Germanic migrations, as discussed above. Changes in dress style in the fifth century could therefore equally show a rapid adoption of 'Germanic' fashion by the native population, who had after all adapted to Roman culture, and would perhaps find Germanic culture more recognisable because of the common 'Celtic' heritage (some Celtic dress fashions lingered on within the Empire until at least the second century AD, and could have been kept alive through folk memory beyond this time). The Celtic resurgence of jewellery and decorative style at the end of the Roman Empire and in the Dark Ages was mentioned in the opening chapter of this book. However, it is also the case that styles of dress before the Roman conquest were very similar to those which were worn by the Germanic tribes which were passing through or settling within the Empire towards its end.

Throughout the life of the Roman Empire, the Germanic tribes living beyond the frontier merely continued to wear the same type of dress they had always been wearing. In the pre-Roman period, this was a pan-European 'Celtic' fashion. It was eventually replaced within the empire by a different style of dress, which could be described as ' provincial Roman'. A 'Celtic resurgence' when Roman authority ceased could therefore also have been encouraged by the parallel changes to a Germanic dress style which was similar to Celtic dress worn before the Roman conquest. The emphasis is on the influence of cultures which were not 'Roman'. When viewed in the long term, so-called 'provincial Roman' dress style seems to have been a temporary aberration for a few centuries in the middle of an otherwise very long-lived tradition.

Though Roman dress styles, especially women's dress, seem not to have survived for very long anywhere, on the Continent many Roman aspects of culture continued, and changes introduced by the Romans were more permanent. Towns, for example, continued in occupation, and presumably still functioned as redistribution centres. Many cities on the Continent do not provide us with much archaeological evidence, but that is because they have continued to be lived in from the Roman period to the present, and we have not had the chance to dig beneath our feet in search of the evidence. Where the floors of cathedrals and churches have been excavated, there are invariably Roman churches beneath. The glass industry, based in the Rhineland, was apparently totally unaffected by any changes at the end of the fourth century, despite the intensive military activity in this area. It continued to make vessels which were based on fourth-century Roman styles, gradually drifting away from this towards the production of new forms. One particular Rhenish pottery industry, making Mayen ware (made from the clay found locally, and very characteristic), continued with the production of pottery in an unbroken sequence from the Roman period until the fourteenth century. Not only did the potters continue to use the same site, but many of the styles of vessel also remained unchanged. There was therefore no marked disruption in many spheres of life and culture. Roman-derived culture survived in numerous aspects of life. In France, where the Franks considered themselves to be the direct inheritors of Roman authority, churches, towns, religion, language, law, pottery and glassware all survived in a more or less recognisable form. In Britain, by contrast, settled by less Romanized Angles, Saxons, and Jutes, long lasting Roman influence is much less apparent.

What results from this investigation of the end of the Roman Empire? Some concrete changes in both civilian and military culture in the fourth century were certainly significant in the final years of Roman authority. Each different region of the Western Empire has its own preferences in Roman-style dress, and in burial rites. Objects worn by people in their everyday lives provide an insight into their society and culture and are often linked to the expression of a particular identity. Changes in those objects will map cultural change, even if the underlying cause remains elusive. Sometimes, we can even look at how the symbolic function of objects worn appears to change. Objects which were once only worn by Germanic people seem to become normal items of provincial Roman culture. Objects which were once military become items of civilian dress.

An 'End' of a kind is demonstrable from the material in the ground as well as from the historical sources. Activity on the frontiers, for example, can be clearly demonstrated. We can even look at changes in occupation on the frontiers through material culture. Combining the evidence from dress accessories, burial customs and other practices, we can show that for some, encounters with foreign travellers and barbarians were an everyday reality.

However, the End of the Roman Empire, as has often been pointed out, is a misleading term to use for the changes at the end of the fourth century and in the fifth century. The end of official Roman authority would perhaps be more accurate. The end of some types of Roman culture, but the survival of others. Why some survive and others do not is a fascinating question.

Germanic influence on Roman culture, particularly in dress, began well before the official end of the West. Some aspects of Roman culture continued well beyond it. The material record shows a process of ongoing development and transformation through the early medieval period and beyond. By the time the Roman Empire ended in the West, it had already altered out of all recognition, and was perhaps no longer even 'Roman' at all.

Selected museums

Museums tend to vary the objects on display, but all of these museums have significant collections of the artefacts mentioned in this book.

Britain

British Museum
The department of Prehistoric and Romano-British Antiquities has material from London, sites in the south-east, such as Colchester, and odd finds from further afield, like the crossbow brooch found in the Moray Firth in Scotland.

Museum of London
The museum has collections of material from more recent excavations in London, particularly the Roman cemeteries.

Arbeia Roman Fort, South Shields
The museum, based at the fort on Hadrian's wall, contains objects and other material found at Arbeia and other sites along the wall.

Canterbury, The Roman Museum
The grave goods from the Stour Street pit burial are on display in the museum, together with other local late Roman material.

Winchester Museum and the Hyde Historic Resource Centre, Winchester
Selected finds from the Lankhills cemetery are on display at the museum, with the full collection stored at the resource centre. The museum also contains other finds from Winchester and the surrounding area.

Belgium

Gallo-Romeins Museum, Tongeren
Tongeren was the Roman capital of the province of Germania Inferior, and the museum has correspondingly large and impressive collections of material from Tongeren and its environs.

Musée Archéologique, Tournai

This museum has collections of jewellery from the fifth century and later, as well as Roman material from the extensive excavations of cemetery sites in Tournai.

Museés Royaux d'Art et d' Histoire, Brussels

A variety of material from Tournai, Tongeren and other important Roman sites in Belgium.

France

Musée des Antiquités et d' Archéologie, Strasbourg

The collections include material from the Roman cemeteries excavated in Strasbourg in the nineteenth century.

Musée des Antiquités Nationales, Saint Germain-en-Laye

Many interesting finds from both the late Roman and Frankish periods are on display in the museum, which has an excellent collection of material, much of it recovered by nineteenth century antiquarians surveying the départements of northern France. There are also some finds held here which were made by Napoleon III and his entourage in the Fôret de Compiègne.

Germany

Rheinisches Landesmuseum Trier

Trier is perhaps the most important site in the area covered by this book, and the museum only displays a fraction of the Roman material in its collection. This does, however, include some of the more impressive gold crossbow brooches found at Trier.

Römisch-Germanisch Zentralmuseum Mainz

A prestigious museum with an strong research record for the study of the Roman provinces in Germany. A part of the records and collections were destroyed in the Second World War, but the museum still has an impressive display of Roman dress accessories and other artefacts.

Römisch-Germanisch Museum Köln (Cologne)

A particularly important museum for the study of Roman glass, but many brooches and other objects are also found in the collections.

Holland

GM Kam Museum Nijmegen

Nijmegen, the site of a Roman fort, houses one of the largest Continental collections of crossbow brooches, which were a topic of particular interest to a former director of the museum, Dr. Van Buchems. Current excavations of Roman cemeteries in Nijmegen are continuing to bring up large amounts of material, and much of it is on display here.

Luxembourg

Musée d' Histoire et d'art, Luxembourg

Though Luxembourg is a small country it contains the large Roman town of Dalheim, which has yielded a wealth of material over the years. Many of the objects from this site and other places in Luxembourg are displayed at the museum and housed in its back room collections.

Further reading

There are numerous books published about different aspects of the later Roman Empire. Some general reading is given below, followed by more detailed references for each chapter.

General

Jones, A.H.M. 1973 *The Later Roman Empire 285-602: a social and economic survey,* Blackwell, Oxford, is the definitive work on the late Roman period for a basic summary of historical events.

Jones, M. 1996 *The End of Roman Britain,* Cornell University Press, London, is a recent publication dealing with the end of the Roman Empire from the perspective of just one province.

Kagan ed. 1992 *The End of the Roman Empire: decline or transformation,* Lexington, Massachusets, looks at the end of the Roman Empire generally, from a more historical perspective.

Swift 2000 'Regionality in dress accessories in the late Roman West', *Monographies Instrumentum* no. 11., Éditions Monique Mergoil, Montagnac, is the publication of my thesis, for exhaustive detail on most of the topics covered in this book.

1 Introduction

Anderson, W. B. 1980 ed. & trans. *Sidonius Appolinaris, Poems and Letters,* 2 volumes, Loeb Classical Library, Harvard University Press, London, the English translation of the original historical source written in fifth century Gaul, is probably one of the most informative contemporary documents. Some of it is very turgid (especially the poems, which should be avoided at all costs) but there are some fascinating details about Germanic overlords and Gallo-Roman society.

Böhme, H. 1974 'Germanische Grabfunde des 4 bis 5 Jahrhunderts', *Münchner Beitrage zur Vor-und-Frühgeschichte* 19, C.H. Beck, Munchen, gives the original dating sequence.

Böhme, H. 1987 'Gallien in der Spatantike', *Jahrbuch des Römischen-Germanischen Zentralmuseums zu Mainz* 34, 770-73, sets out the evidence for Böhmes revised dating sequence for Continental sites.

Hope-Taylor, B. 1977 *Yeavering, an Anglo-British centre of early Northumbria*, HMSO, London, is the site report of a settlement with evidence for both Roman and Anglo-Saxon influence in architectural style.

James, E. 1988 *The Franks*, Blackwell, Oxford, is a good introduction to this group of barbarians. Other volumes in the same series (*The Peoples of Europe*) are also interesting.

Pitt-Rivers, W. 1887–1905 *Excavations in Cranborne Chase*, near Rushmore, on the borders of Dorset and Wilts., privately printed, London, published in 5 volumes, is a report on his excavation of Roman and prehistoric sites. Antiquarian books can be difficult to find, but these volumes may be slightly more available in Britain and give an idea of nineteenth century scholarship.

2 Dress, identity and regionality in the provinces

Bland, R. & Johns, C., 1993 *The Hoxne Treasure: an illustrated introduction*, British Museum Press, London.

Burger, A. 1966 'The Late Roman Cemetery at Sagvar', *Acta Archaeologia Akademiai Scientarum Hungaricae* 18, 99-234, is a publication in English which shows the late Roman burial practice in Hungary.

Bruce-Mitford, 1983 *The Sutton Hoo Ship burial*, 'Late Roman and Byzantine Silver, Hanging Bowls, Drinking Vessels, Cauldrons and other containers, textiles, the lyre, pottery bottle and other items', Volume 3, (Care-Evans, A. ed. 1983). The Trustees of the British Museum, British Museum Publications, London. This volume, as its rather unwieldy title suggests, is primarily a finds catalogue of some of the material from Sutton Hoo, and is a good introduction to the specifics of finds analysis, with several excellent specialist reports.

Cooke, N. 1999 unpublished University of London PhD thesis, is a survey of late Roman cemeteries in north-western Europe, specifically with more detail on military burial rites

Cool, H. 1983 *A Study of the Roman Personal Ornaments made of metal*, unpublished PhD. thesis, University of Wales, Cardiff, is a compilation and study of all types of metal jewellery except brooches found in southern Britain.

Cool, H. 1992 'Roman metal hair pins from Southern Britain', *The Archaeological Journal* 147, 148-82, shows the regional distribution of various pin types.

Cunliffe, B. ed. 1988, *The Temple of Sulis Minerva at Bath volume 2: the finds from the sacred spring*, Oxford University Committee for Archaeology, Oxford, is the site report publication of the small finds.

Eicher, J. ed. 1995 Dress and Ethnicity, Berg, Oxford, and Shennan 1989, *Archaeological Approaches to Cultural Identity*, Unwin Hyman, London, cover the symbolism of dress and dress accessories, and how people construct identity through dress and other means.

Guido, M. 1979 'Glass beads of the Prehistoric and Roman periods in Britain and Ireland, Society of Antiquaries Research Report' 35, Society of Antiquaries, London, is the definitive work on beads in Britain, with a catalogue of beads found at sites and discussion of typology etc.

Heurgon, J. 1958 *Le Tresor de Ténès*, Arts & Metiers Graphiques, Paris, is the publication of the precious metal hoard, including openwork gold bracelets and gold type 7 crossbow brooches.

Johns, C. 1996 *The Jewellery of Roman Britain*, UCL press, London, gives a good overview of general jewellery fashions in the province. Other books which deal with the more common types of dress accessories are quite difficult to find; anything with 'jewellery' in the title usually sticks to gold and silver, mostly too early.

Johns, C. 1997 *The Snettisham Roman Jeweller's Hoard*, British Museum Press, London, is a fascinating study of the hoard of a second-century jeweller, including detailed anlayses of the metal jewellery and intaglios found in the hoard.

Keller, E. 1979 'Die spätrömische Grabfunde in Sudbayern', *Münchner Beitrage zur Vor- und-Frühgeschichte* 14, C.H. Beck, Munchen, is an invaluable compilation of cemeteries and smaller sites with burials in South Bavaria, Germany, including Keller's original crossbow brooch typology.

Mertens, J. & Van Impe, L. 1971 'Het Laat Romeins Graafveld van Oudenburg', *Archaeologia Belgica* 135, Brussel, is the publication of the large and important Roman fort and cemetery on the channel coast of Belgium.

Pröttel, P. 1988 'Zur Chronologie der Zwiebelknopffiblen', *Jahrbuch der Römisch-Germanisch ZentralMuseum Mainz* 35, 347-72, is Pröttel's revision of Keller's original typology.

Sebesta, J. & Bonfante, L. eds. 1994 *The World of Roman Costume*, University of Wisconsin Press, Madison is about more general aspects of Roman dress. The information about the changing symbolism of the toga is taken from a paper in this volume.

Stone, S. 1994, 'The Toga: from national to ceremonial costume,' in Sebesta and Bonfante eds. *The World of Roman Costume*, University of Wisconsin Press, Madison.

Tempelmann-Macyzynska, M. 1985 'Perlen im Mitteleuropäisch Barbaricum', *Römisch-Germanisch Forschungen* Band 43, Philipp Von Zabern, Mainz, is a study of beads beyond the frontiers of the Roman Empire.

Wheeler, R.E.M. & Wheeler, T.V. 1932, *Report on the Excavation of the prehistoric and Romano site at Lydney Park*, is the site report for the temple at Lydney, though only a selection of the deposit of bracelets found are published here. The bracelets themselves are in a private collection.

146

Woodward and Leach 1993 *The Uley Shrines*, English Heritage/ British Museum Press, London, is the site report on excavations at Uley, and has an extensive discussion of temple rital deposits.

3 People travelling in late Antiquity

Bayley, J. 1992 *Non-ferrous metalworking in England, Late Iron Age to Early Medieval*, unpublished PH.D thesis, University of London, covers evidence for the production of metal objects as well as scientific analysis of the Richborough crossbow brooches.

Bennet, P. 1980 '68-69a' Stour Street, *Archaeologia Cantiana* XCVI, 406-10 reports on the discovery of the Stour Street pit burial. The finds are currently being written up and should be published relatively soon.

Böhme, H. 1974 'Germanische Grabfunde des 4 bis 5 Jahrhunderts', *Münchner Beitrage zur Vor-und-Frühgeschichte* 19, C.H. Beck, Munchen, is a benchmark study of grave finds of the fourth and fifth centuries between the Loire in France and the Elbe in Germany; covering both the Roman West and Germanic homelands outside the frontiers.

Boon, G. 1977 'Gold in Glass beads from the ancient World', *Britannia* 8, 193-207, discusses the possible source for this bead type and their chemical analysis.

Burger, A. 1979 *Das Spätrömische Graberfeld von Somogyszil*, Akademiai Kiado, Budapest, is a typical Hungarian cemetery, with plans of the graves clearly showing the distinctive female burial rite.

Clarke 1979 'The Roman Cemetery at Lankhills', *Winchester Studies* 3, Clarendon Press, Oxford, is the site report of the excavation. Clarke discusses in detail the foreign graves from the site.

Farwell, D. & Molleson, T. 1993 *Excavations at Poundbury 1966-80 volume 2: The Cemeteries*, Dorset Natural History & Archaeology Society Monograph Series 11, Dorchester, is the site report of the excavation.

Halsall, G. 1992 'The origin of the Reihengräberzivilisation: 40 years on', 196-207 in Drinkwater & Eltham eds. *Fifth century Gaul: A Crisis of Identity*, Cambridge University Press, Cambridge, discusses the fifth-century burials with new types of grave ritual in northern France and Belgium. Other papers in the edited volume are also interesting and useful for this region in the fifth century.

James, E. 1977 'The Merovingian Archaeology of south-west Gaul', *British Archaeological Reports Supplementary Series* 25, Oxford, looks at the early medieval period in France.

Marin, J. 1990, *Attilla: Les influences Danubiennes dans l'ouest de l'Europe au Ve siècle* discusses the foreign burials at Fontenay and the Attilla myth through the centuries. A more detailed examination of the cemetery at Fontenay is provided by the site report, including full details of the physical anthropolgy of the skeletons found at Fontenay:

Pilet, C. 1994 *La Necropole de Saint-Martin-de-Fontenay, Calvados, 54e supplement à Gallia*, CNRS Editions, Paris.

Pirling, R. 1974 'Das römische-frankische Graberfeld von Krefeld-Gellep', *Denkmaler der Volkerwanderungzeit* Serie B Band 8, Gebr. Mann, Berlin.

Pirling, R. 1979 'Das römische-frankische Graberfeld von Krefeld-Gellep', *Denkmaler der Volkerwanderungzeit* Serie B Band 10, Gebr. Mann, Berlin.

Pirling, R. 1989 'Das römische-frankische Graberfeld von Krefeld-Gellep', *Denkmaler der Volkerwanderungzeit* Serie B Band 13, Franz Steiner, Wiesbaden.

Pirling, R. 1966 'Das römische-frankische Graberfeld von Krefeld-Gellep', *Denkmaler der Volkerwanderungzeit* Serie B Band 2, Gebr. Mann, Berlin.

Pirling, R. 1997 'Das römische-frankische Graberfeld von Krefeld-Gellep 1975-82', *Denkmaler der Volkerwanderungzeit* Serie B Band 17, Franz Steiner, Wiesbaden.
These collected volumes, still in progress, form the site report for the massive late Roman and Frankish cemetery of Krefeld-Gellep, which is a very good starting point for any study of material of the late Roman and early medieval periods.

Riha, E. 1990 'Der römische Schmuck aus Augst und Kaiseraugst, Forschungen' in *Augst 10, Römermuseum Augst*, Augst, is a catalogue of Roman jewellery found at Augst, including bracelets and beads. The brooches are published separately in the following volumes:

Riha, E. 1979 'Die römischen Fibeln aus Augst and Kaiseraugst', Forschungen in *Augst 3, Romermuseum Augst*, Augst.

Riha, E. 1994 'Die römischen Fibeln aus Augst und Kaiseraugst:' Die Neufunde seit 1975, Forschungen in *Augst 18, Romermuseum Augst*, Augst.

Tempelmann Macynzska 1985, *Perlen in mitteleuropäischen Barbaricum*, full reference given above, is a study of beads beyond the frontiers, with distribution maps of each different type.

Vanvinckenroye, W. 1984 *De Romeinse Zuidwest Begraafplaatz van Tongeren*, Provincial Gallo-Romeins Museum, Tongeren, is probably the most widely available excavation report for cemeteries of the important Roman town of Tongeren.

4 Army movements and the collapse of the frontier

Cunliffe, B. 1975 *Excavations at Portchester Castle*, vol. 1 Roman, Society of Antiquaries research report 32, Society of Antiquaries, London, is the site report of the Roman fort. Der Romische Limes in Osterrreich, for example, which covers the area running through Austria.

King, A. 1990 *Roman Gaul and Germany*, British Museum Publications, London, gives a summary of the limes frontier in English, though for a really detailed and up to date study German scholarship must be referred to, in particular the proceedings of the 'LimesKongress' conferences.

King, C. 1992 'Roman, local and barbarian coinages in fifth century Gaul', 184-95 in Drinkwater & Eltham eds. *Fifth century Gaul: a crisis of identity*, Cambridge University Press, Cambridge, is a study of coin types and distributions around the Meuse and other areas.

Mertens, J. 1977 'Quelques considerations sur le limes Belgicus', *Akten des XI Internationalen LimesKongress*, 63-81, Akademiai Kiado, Budapest, discusses the question of the Roman frontier in the Rhine delta/Meuse area.

Sommer, M. 1984 *Die Gürtel und Gürtelbeschlage des 4 und 5 Jahrhunderts im Römischen Reich*, Bonner Hefte zur Vorgeschichte 22, Bonn, is a study of late Roman buckles and belt fittings throughout the whole of Europe, with a very detailed typology and full catalogue.

Southern & Dixon 1996 *The Late Roman Army*, Batsford, London, is a good place to start for a general overview of the army in the late Roman period.

5 The end of the West and beyond

Brulet 1995 *La Sépulture du roi Childeric à Tournai et le site funéraire*, Université de Louvain, Louvain-la-neuve, is the most up to date excavation report on Childeric's grave, which has been published several times since its discovery in the 17th century.

Dasnoy, A. 1967 'Le cimetière a Éprave', *Annales de la Société des Antiquaires de Namur* 54, 61-105, is the site report of the cemetery of Éprave in Belgium, with burials containing worn personal ornaments and weapons.

Dombay, J. 1956 *Der Götische Grabfund von Domolospuszta*, A Janus Pannonius Museums Evk. vol 1 (unnumbered series) 104-30, is the publication of grave finds from the site.

Koch, U. 1969 'Alamannisch Gräber des ersten Halfte des 6 Jahrhunderts', *Bayerische Vorgeschichtesblatter* 34, 62-93, lists and discusses silver 'Kolbenarmringe' from the sixth century, in particular the way in which they were worn, and their grave associations with other high status material.

Robinson, G. 1914 ed. & trans. *Eugippius, the Life of Saint Severinus*, Harvard University Press, Cambridge, is the English translation of the original historical source for the Roman province of Noricum (present day Austria), which mentions the manufacture of gold objects.

Thorpe, L. 1974 ed. & trans. *Gregory of Tours: The History of the Franks*, Penguin, London, is the English translation in the Penguin Classics series of the original historical source, and contains lots of interesting background material on the Franks, though Gregory of Tours is writing too late to be a prime source for the fifth century.

Van Driel Murray, C. 1987 *Roman footwear: a mirror of fashion and society*, Friendship-Taylor, Swann & Thomas eds. Recent Research in archaeological footwear, Association of Archaeological Illustrators and Surveyors, London, covers in depth the changes in Roman footwear styles throughout the Roman period.

Werner, J. 1980 'Der goldene Armring des Frankenkönigs Childerich und die germanischen Handgelenkringe der jungeren Kaiserzeit', *Frühmittelaltliche Studien* 14, 1-49, catalogues gold Kolbenarmringe from the third and fifth centuries and discusses their metal composition and distribution in the Roman Empire and in free Germany.

You should be able to find most of these books in a good university library; translations of historical sources and a couple of the more general books will also be available more widely.

Index

Figures in **bold** indicate text illustrations